Praise 1

"This is an easy-to-understand book on the practicalities of dealing with pain, showing clearly 'why struggles make relationships stronger.' It is appetizing and, at the same time, offers solid instruction to anyone who feels a desire to face the adversities that life brings."

FATHER FRANCIS KABIRU
Pastor, St. Agnes Catholic Church

"Steve Ritter is a highly-respected counselor known for his empathy, insight and pragmatism. His new book, 'Useful Pain,' makes it clear that strong relationships are never easy. He helps you understand that every relationship has its challenges, and that there are practical steps you can take to move through the challenges to an even richer relationship."

GAIL R. MENELEY
Co-Founder, Shields Meneley Partners, Chicago, Illinois

"Before you throw in the towel, read this book! Too many couples quit before they really understand what's going on in their relationship. Steve reassures the reader that there are missteps and failures in every relationship and that these are precisely what is required to move couples to deeper intimacy and authenticity. The couples highlighted are like us, or someone we know, making this book especially accessible, practical and encouraging. This is excellent advice for relationships in all stages of growth."

REV. JEANNE HANSON
Executive Director,
Samaritan Counseling Center of the Northwest Suburbs

"This book offers a clear and easily understandable journey through the cycles of our intimate relationships. It builds self-awareness and thus provides a useful framework to take our relationships to the next level. A must-read for anyone at any stage of their relationship."

ALAN R. GRAHAM, PhD, PCC, MCAC
ACP Consultants, Ltd

"So often in life, we encounter difficult situations involving our relationships with others. We can choose to walk away from these relationships or to remain in them. If we chose the latter, it will require that we struggle with the pain of making that relationship better. The result is also a stronger relationship. In his first book, 'Team Clock: A Guide To Breakthrough Teams,' Steve Ritter introduces us to the Team Clock approach to addressing and resolving interpersonal conflict and barriers in a way that results in stronger and more productive and rewarding relationships. In his new book, 'Useful Pain: Why Your Relationships Need Struggle,' Steve brings these powerful tools to more personal relationships helping to strengthen the bond between couples, families, and friends so they can function together as a team and achieve their goals too whatever they might be."

JOSEPH R. ZANDER, Ph.D.
Assistant Clinical Professor, Department of Psychiatry
University of Illinois, Chicago

"In today's complex world, there are those who would encourage our impulse to avoid struggle and conflict in our daily lives so our paths are always "stress free and painless." Yet, the greatest teachers, coaches and mentors advise the opposite. Anything valuable that we either gain or grow into cannot be accomplished without struggle, sacrifice or pain. Steve Ritter's latest book shows us how to embrace struggle in order to grow in insight, empathy for others and mastery of our talents."

PRISCILLA HERBISON, MSW, JD
Professor, St. Mary's University

"Steve shows how much he values and wants to strengthen relationships with his new book. He uses thoughtful stories to illustrate common experiences in relationships along with good insights and useful strategies. Couples can learn more about themselves and each other, and increase their level of communication, fun and energy. It is refreshingly positive, enthusiastic and motivating. This is an excellent resource for couples at any stage of their relationship, whether it be in their early courtship, married for many years or somewhere in between."

MICHAEL WAGNER, M.D.
Founder, Performance Enhancement Coaching

"Informed by psychological/developmental theory, clinical research and a wealth of knowledge derived from over thirty years of practice, Steve Ritter's Useful Pain offers the reader an excellent guide for salvaging, enhancing, and deepening the relationship of the couple in myriad ways."

RANDOLPH LUCENTE, Ph. D.
Professor, Loyola University of Chicago School of Social Work

"Steve aptly intertwines the principles that apply to creating healthy work groups into the principles of creating a successful marriage. While it should be obvious that the principles are exactly the same, how easy it is to take marriage for granted while investing immense energy in the workplace."

GINGER BARTHEL
Senior Consultant, Borling and Associates

"Which romantic relationship has known no struggle? This book helps every couple understand the difficulties they face more thoroughly, and live up to the challenges more constructively. Full of stories we can all identify with, it is an easy read that's well worth the hour or two you'll invest. Save yourself headaches, heartaches and heartbreaks, then use it to help those you love as well!"

MARIE-JOSÉE SHAAR, MAPP, CPT
Wellness Speaker, Consultant and Facilitator.
Author of Smarts and Stamina: The Busy Person's Guide to Optimal Health and Performance.

"Useful Pain *will fundamentally change how you think about your own relationship challenges and rewards. Filled with evocative examples, Steve has taken the complexity of personal partnerships and turned it into a simple roadmap of endless exploration - marked by new ways of relating. It has encouraged me to apply this practical wisdom and sustainable technique to enhance my own life. A 'must-read!'"*

TINA A. HAUBERT
Managing Director, The Executives' Club of Chicago

"A very practical, succinct, and hands-on guide about how to navigate complex human relationships."

NADINE KELLY, M.D.
Yogi MD

"Useful Pain *is readable, practical and straightforward for the lay person, as well as professionals. The stages provide a great framework to use in exploring and evaluating the quality and opportunity in our relationships. Each challenge presents great opportunity when we have the tools to understand, evaluate, and communicate with our loved ones."*

ANN C. SCHREINER, LCSW
President and CEO, Pillars

"There indeed are no days off in relationships. This book, truly fit for any and all relationships, teaches us how to ensure that each day helps us live out our happily ever after. A great and necessary read."

ELVISA PANDZIC
Research Analyst, Networked Insights

"Steve has the ability to transcend his skills in impressive and sensitive ways to positively impact challenges that all partners face. In an easy to follow process, Steve shares his intrinsic and sophisticated way of intervening which allows us all to take our relationships to the next level."

JACKI FITZGERALD FREDERKING
Dean of Students, Alan B. Shepard High School

"*Useful Pain provides readers with a refreshingly new way to look and think about the pain and/or challenges that arise within interpersonal relationships. The section "ten common challenges of relationships" provides detailed real life examples of how to use the ten challenges to rejuvenate and enhance one's relationships.*"
—ERIKA LINDSTROM
Social Worker, Lexington Medical Center

"*Useful Pain reminds us that it is possible to transform our times of struggle and helps us to understand the cyclical nature of relationships.*"
—MICHELLE MISHLER FRANK, M.D.
Owner/President, Frank Psychiatry

USEFUL PAIN

"*Useful Pain* reminds us that it is possible to transform our times of struggle and helps us to understand the cyclical nature of relationships."

MICHELLE MISHLER FRANK, M.D. Owner/President, Frank Psychiatry

AUTHOR OF
TEAM CLOCK®
A Guide to
Breakthrough Teams

USEFUL PAIN

**WHY
YOUR
RELATIONSHIPS
NEED
STRUGGLE**

STEVE RITTER

For bulk orders, please call 630.832.6155
or email booksales@teamclock.com

Copyright © 2014 by Team Clock Institute.
All Rights Reserved.
Cover art copyright © 2014, cover design, and interior layout design by Weykyoi Victor Kore

Published by Team Clock® Institute.

All rights reserved. No part of this publication may be reproduced, stored in a retrieval system or transmitted in any form or by any means – electronic, mechanical, photocopy, recording, or any other – except for brief quotations in printed reviews, without the prior permission of the publisher and contributors.

ISBN 978-1495958137

www.teamclock.com

Printed In The United States of America.

Dedication

Useful Pain *is dedicated to my mom, Helen Elizabeth Ritter (Betts), who devoted her life to lifting others with kindness, love, grace, and resilience.*

Contents

Foreword   1
Take Your Relationships to the Next Level

Introduction   3
Why Relationships Get Stuck

Chapter One   11
The Natural and Necessary Cycle
of Every Relationship

Chapter Two   47
Discovery

Chapter Three   55
Intimacy

Chapter Four   65
Adventure

Chapter Five — 75
Space

Chapter Six — 121
Moving Relationships Forward
The Ten Common Challenges of Relationships

Afterword — 127
Now What?

Appendix — 129
Resources

Foreword

In my last book, *Team Clock: A Guide to Breakthrough Teams*, I provided a simple model for creating and sustaining effective teams. As I shared the Team Clock concept with individuals, educators, small business owners, and Fortune 500 companies, time and again people asked me how these principles applied to interpersonal relationships. Could the conflict resolution and team building strategies applied in the boardroom also work in the bedroom? Does the cycle of distancing and trust play out between couples and management teams alike? The answer is, "Yes!"

Through the following pages, I will provide you with a time-tested tool to lift all the relationships in your life to the next level. As a husband, father, teacher, and social worker, I offer a blend of clinical, educational, and family expertise to the conversation. Both personally and professionally, I have seen thousands of relationships advance to more satisfying levels of connection.

Look back at your history, take stock of your current circumstances, and look ahead to new possibilities. We all have themes and patterns that shape our most significant relationships. Our challenge is to find the courage to strengthen what works well and to adjust what doesn't. Every interaction counts. With each word, decision, and action, we move our most precious relationships either toward or away from wellness.

Introduction

It took three tries for Sara and Hank to become a couple. They dated initially in high school when all their friends were sampling romance for the first time. Fueled partially by adolescent lust, the chemistry was strong. As teenagers, days were filled with flirting and nights included some sexual discovery. They did everything together. Sara and Hank intentionally applied to the same colleges believing they would stay together. Neither anticipated the breakup when they both accepted offers from the University of Minnesota.

Wired with distinct personalities, their differences became obstacles as they transitioned from adolescence to adulthood. Sara's nature was quiet and reserved. Hank was opinionated and direct. In social circles, Hank dominated conversations, while Sara valued the art of listening. The rhythms of flirtation were now spliced with conflict. They were slowly moving away from each other.

Before leaving for college and after much deliberation, Sara decided to break up with Hank. Although she had mixed feelings, Sara believed it would be best for both of them. Ambivalently, Hank agreed with Sara's decision. He had no other dating experience and, truth be told, was looking forward to arriving on the Minneapolis campus unattached. Sara, too, was excited about the chance to meet new people.

A large urban campus was an easy place to get lost in a new lifestyle. Sara and Hank ran into each other from time to time but had limited interaction at school. Routine trips home for the holidays provided a chance to catch up as they coordinated transportation between the Twin Cities and their suburban Chicago homes. Seven-hour car rides allowed ample opportunity to hear about each other's classes, the latest shenanigans at fraternity and sorority parties, and new romantic interests. The road trips were comfortable and fun.

Four years passed quickly. Sara and Hank established a solid friendship. Sara grew to appreciate Hank's energy and Hank became fond of Sara's thoughtfulness. Sara was confident Hank would find a stable career in business and eventually pursue a graduate degree. Hank imagined Sara finding happiness in a role blending a job with her psychology degree, her love for volunteering, and her devotion to family. Life was moving forward favorably for each of them.

It wasn't until the end of their senior year that they discovered a renewed romantic interest in each other. Sara recently ended a brief fling with a graduate assistant who would soon accept a teaching offer from the university. She intended to return to Chicago after graduation and was not interested in navigating a long-distance relationship. Hank had been unattached for the majority of his senior year as the woman he dated through most of his college years had met someone else and unceremoniously announced a split. Both Sara and Hank were newly single.

The rides from Minneapolis to Chicago and back to the Twin Cities during their senior-year spring break held the magic of a first date. It was as though five years of history rushed to the present. Conversation flowed with ease. Looking ahead, they were eager for the chance to be together more regularly after completing their college degrees. A few months later, Sara and Hank helped each other pack up four years of memories for the next stage of life.

Days turned to weeks and weeks became months. Gradually, their connection became firmly rooted as Sara and Hank began to consider a future together. By now, they shared many things in common despite the fundamental differences in their personalities. They knew each other deeply. They would both be launching from their family homes and starting new careers. Most importantly, they genuinely enjoyed each other's company. Deciding to move in together was a natural evolution.

Sara and Hank landed jobs quickly. They found an apartment in a part of the city close to work and friends. Learning how to coexist was their next challenge. Once Sara and Hank moved in together, the realities of sharing space, household responsibilities, schedules, and lifestyles seemed to ignite their differences. Enduring each other's habits and *eccentricities was difficult. Sometimes, the quirks were endearing. Other times, they found each other's idiosyncrasies annoying.*

Joining lives turned out to be a bigger test than building a friendship and falling in love. The most potent aspects of their personalities became magnified. When they disagreed, Hank became aggressive and insistent. Sara became moody and distant. As this pattern repeated, Hank and Sara grew weary of the extended periods of tension and the mounting list of unresolved issues.

Eventually, the daily discomfort arising from the stockpile of hurts forced them to reexamine their coping styles. They realized their natural instincts were repelling them away from each other rather than bringing them closer together. To have any hope of staying together, they would need to learn how to understand each other's perspective and negotiate compromise. This would be a lot of work.

Starting with the little things, Sara and Hank inserted a timeout into their arguments to settle the intensity of the moment. Once calm, they stopped to clarify whatever issue was on the table. They then engaged in the exercise of naming their partner's position in an effort to better understand each other's frame of reference. They made certain to double-check their understandings to ensure they weren't moving forward with any misperceptions.

Once both viewpoints had been aired, they weighed the pros and cons of each option and tried to identify a com-

promise solution. The compromise was rarely an even split between each person's wishes. Most often, it resulted in one of them deferring to the other's preference which was much easier when both sides had been acknowledged.

Hank and Sara gradually lifted their relationship to a new level. Their natural inclination to attack or retreat under pressure became a signal to employ their new techniques. Hank learned to step back and be more patient. Sara learned to speak up and be more assertive. Most importantly, they learned how to avoid hurting each other and how to repair damage when injury occurred.

Collaboration replaced stubbornness. Occasional lapses led to old, unsuccessful coping efforts but, overall, the relationship worked. As the one-year anniversary of moving in together approached, both Sara and Hank had grown in maturity. No longer two individuals battling for turf, they were now a couple with mutual goals.

Over time, the couple gained traction and momentum. Daily routines further anchored their coping strengths as norms. Sara and Hank discovered a recipe for solving problems. It leveraged the best of both of their personalities and capitalized on the richness of their differences.

They made each other a better person. Neither of them was asking the other to change for them. Both Sara and Hank were asking themselves to grow up for each other. Hank knew he needed to be less rash. Sara understood she needed to be more willing to share her feelings. The new normal felt good.

Hank was the first to suggest an engagement. Sara didn't hesitate. She wanted to spend the rest of her life with Hank.

Their struggle became fuel for growth. There would be plenty of new challenges to tackle as marriage gave way to kids and career paths unveiled critical opportunities. Looking ahead, Sara and Hank would need to apply the lessons of their crisis to the bigger decisions. Should we buy a house? How should we spend our vacation time? How much money should we save or invest? How should we best stretch our holiday commitments to both families? When should we have kids?

The future was certain to unfurl new struggles. While they were unsure of the direction life would take, they trusted the foundation of their relationship. Sara and Hank knew this underpinning was strong enough to support whatever challenges might follow. It was a new beginning.

WHY RELATIONSHIPS GET STUCK

Fun and intimacy are the parts of a relationship most of us anticipate when we form a connection and imagine a future with another person. It feels good to think about these possibilities. It feels even better to experience them. Fun and intimacy, however, are always balanced by struggle and challenge. People grow. Circumstances change. Partnerships evolve.

It's usually the small, annoying things that create friction. But sometimes, it's more serious. Occasionally, the foundation of the relationship gets fractured by the recently discovered infidelity, the late-night pornography habit, or the out-of-control addiction. Romantic relationships are complex. They're always breaking. As soon as you fix one problem, something else goes wrong. Amidst the fun and the romance are countless variations of heartache.

When a crisis arises, it's normal to want to escape. No one likes pain. When you're in the middle of a struggle, it's hard to see there might be something to be gained. So, we do whatever it takes to get things back to normal, even when "normal" might not be a good solution. Sometimes, it's okay to be in a crisis. It might even be good. Usually, it depends on what you do next.

Often, opportunities are hidden from view.

This is a book about discovering the opportunities that unfold as relationships mature. In the pages ahead, you will learn about the nature of healthy relationships. You will be encouraged to assess the strengths and vulnerabilities of the connections in your life. You will be introduced to a way to evolve – to enhance intimacy and guide your relationships in a healthy direction. Most importantly, you will be invited to follow your opportunities and embrace your challenges as a roadmap to more effective relationships.

This book offers a guide for navigating the real world of romance. You will be introduced to a simple model for healthy relationships in Chapter 1. You will see the model unfold in Chapters 2, 3, 4, and 5. In Chapter 6, you will do a deep dive where you learn ten specific "useful pain" opportunities in relationships.

When you have finished reading this book, you are invited to participate in an exercise. The *Interpersonal Assessment* provides a *Card Sort* to measure the health of your relationship and an *Action Workbook* to help steer the conversations that will strengthen your connection. Carve out some time to sit down with the most important people in your life and take ownership of the wellness and direction of each relationship. Move your connections forward.

Chapter One

The Natural and Necessary Cycle of Every Relationship

Pick an important romantic relationship in your life and think about the times you and your partner have experienced struggles. Perhaps there was a misunderstanding in communication. Possibly trust was violated. One of you might have said or done something disrespectful. There may have been a trauma or a tragedy that altered everything in your lives. Sometimes people grow in different directions and change at different paces. When you blend the unique histories and personalities of two people into a shared connection, both harmony and dissonance are ignited.

Both peace and friction are normal and healthy in a relationship. Each has purpose in helping us grow – individually and as partners. The goal is not to achieve perfection together or to never have conflict. Rather, the goal is to create an environment that supports an adaptable connection where both partners can thrive.

Relationships naturally move through a predictable cycle. As the cycle evolves, four opportunities arise: **Discovery**,

Intimacy, *Adventure*, and *Space*.

A new relationship begins with a stage of *Discovery* where

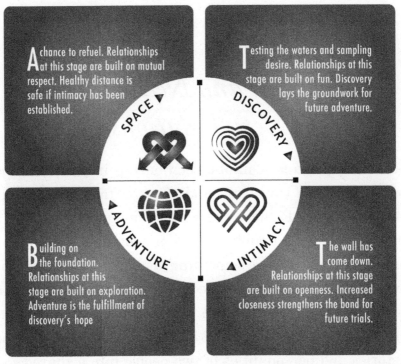

rules, roles, norms, and goals are defined. As the waters are tested, partners learn how conflict and differences are managed. Relationships at this stage are built on fun and desire. Discovery lays the groundwork for future adventure.

From there, partners move to a stage of *Intimacy* where the walls start to come down. A foundation of trust and accountability is established. If this goes well, partners become more cohesive and grow attached. Relationships at this stage are built on openness. Increased closeness strengthens the bond for future trials.

The discovery and intimacy phases create a platform for the ***Adventure*** stage. The connection now evolves to new levels. Relationships at this stage are built on exploration and experimentation. Adventure is the fulfillment of discovery's hope.

The growth created in the Adventure phase requires some adaptation in the ***Space*** stage. Taking a break gives partners a chance to refuel. As the connection finds some distance, changes are negotiated and new circumstances are considered. Relationships at this stage are built on mutual respect. Healthy distance is safe if intimacy has been established. Eventually, this gives way to a renewed stage of discovery as the relationship refocuses on its future realities.

Over time, healthy relationships continue to cycle over and over through renewed stages of *Discovery, Intimacy, Adventure,* and *Space* as the new circumstances get negotiated.

Alex and Dan dated for three years before introducing each other to their families. Dan was concerned about his parents' willingness to accept Alex and wanted to make sure the relationship was committed before exposing his lover and his family to any discomfort. Dan's dad hit it off with Alex immediately. Alex was quickly absorbed into the rhythms and routines of Dan's immediate family.

Things changed when Alex and Dan decided to formalize their vows. The civil ceremony caused a bit of a stir amongst extended family on both sides of the aisle that would have preferred a more traditional arrangement. Both Dan and Alex were now faced with a series of awkward exchanges as they tried to support their partner while defending some of their relatives.

The inconsistency in family support moved from crisis to opportunity. The bond between Dan and Alex was strengthened by each new challenge. Slowly, their families grew to value the strength and resilience the couple showed in the face of adversity. An appreciation for their differences became an anchor in the family system. As the years rolled on, Dan and Alex's marriage served as a model for others. It was grounded. It was close. They took risks. They were resilient.

Looking back, Alex and Dan never expected their connection to evolve from a stigmatized secret to a societal norm. They simply fell in love. Through many cycles of discovery, intimacy, adventure, and space, they elevated their partnership to a level that few couples achieve.

Beginning in each *Discovery* stage, partners reset their

rules of engagement, refine a common direction, and relearn how to agree and disagree. As each *Intimacy* stage recycles, partners advance their capacity for considerate exchange as their closeness grows more warm and familiar. During each *Adventure* stage, the added strength of the attachment allows the relationship to try new challenges and take advantage of the uniqueness of each partner. Finally, each *Space* stage allows partners to let go of what's changed and greet the next round of new possibilities with fresh energy as they enter a renewed, more mature Discovery stage.

The Discovery Stage

Testing the waters and sampling desire: relationships at this stage are built on fun. Discovery lays the groundwork for future adventure.

> *By her thirtieth birthday, Kiera had become more selective about who she was willing to date. The bar scene was old. Most guys seemed to be looking for the same thing – a quick path to a physical relationship with*

as little commitment as possible. Kiera was eager to meet someone different. The odds of finding that rare combination of looks, brains, character, fun, and maturity seemed to be shrinking. When her friend asked Kiera to join her, her boyfriend, and her boyfriend's buddy at a military sponsored ball for returning soldiers, she was willing to give the impromptu foursome a try. Seeing Trevor's picture in uniform only added to the excitement.

The blind date went surprisingly well. Conversation came easily and the dance was fun. The following morning, the four of them went out for breakfast where a spark was evident to both Kiera and Trevor. That night, Kiera's friend called three times to ask whether she liked Trevor or, you know, "liked" him. Kiera tried to conceal her excitement but her friend could hear the anticipation in her tone. Kiera "liked" him.

In the earliest stages, relationships begin slowly as "chemistry" draws a couple together. Two people spend time together simply because they enjoy each other's company. As they grow closer, they establish a few ground rules and test them to make sure they want to move forward. They share a little more of themselves to make sure it's safe to be vulnerable. They mesh important portions of their lives along with a common understanding of where they're headed together.

When Trevor returned to the military base, he went out of his way to make sure Kiera had his contact information. He promised to call regularly and the two of them compared calendars for opportunities to reconnect in person. One of their common interests was a love for baseball. Kiera was a die-hard Detroit Tigers fan and Trevor had grown up rooting for the Cleveland Indians. The natural rivalry stoked some affectionate bantering and gave them two future venues where they could visit each other.

Once they said goodbye and returned to their respective homes, Kiera experienced a surge of anxiety. Their earliest interactions had gone so well. What if he didn't call? Likewise, Trevor wondered whether his connection with Kiera would last. The military lifestyle required frequent moves and his long distance romances had never before survived the promises of the flirtation phase. Trevor vowed to himself that he would do his best to pay attention to Kiera and convince her of his interest. The 170 mile distance between them would mean a heavy reliance on phone calls and text messages. Trevor was determined to keep the momentum going between face-to-face contacts.

At first, the frequency of calls and texts added to the magic of the connection. Kiera kept her phone nearby in anticipation of the next message. With her last boyfriend, Kiera often complained he never called. Now, her phone rang constantly. Trevor was always on her mind and she checked her phone frequently to make sure she hadn't missed a call.

Relationships in the Discovery stage are testing the water – one toe at a time. Each experience is fresh, and new data rolls in with each interaction. Interests and tastes become exposed. Perhaps it's being introduced to new music or a hidden-away restaurant. Maybe it's a probing philosophical discussion on a sensitive issue. Sometimes, it's just the infatuation of noticing each other's uniqueness.

In the beginning, there are more questions than answers. Our imaginations fill in the gaps that experience has yet to unveil. There haven't yet been enough reality-checks to prompt the tough questions - Is this the one? Am I in or out? It will take more evidence to determine if it is "meant to be."

Trevor was enthralled with the budding romance. He wanted to know everything about Kiera. Four or five times each day, Kiera would receive a text message on her phone. "What is your favorite color?" "What is your favorite food?" "If you could go on vacation anywhere in the world, where would you go?" In Trevor's mind, these were conversation-starters. He looked forward to his next visit to Detroit when he and Kiera would go to dinner, take in a ballgame, and continue these talks over a cold beer.

New couples take pleasure in sharing experiences and getting to know each other. Each date provides a preview to the future. Does conversation flow naturally? Does he or she understand my perspective? Am I drained or energized after we spend time together? Excitement builds as partners imagine what might lie ahead. In the near future, companionship now colors the way time will be spent. Looking further ahead, we imagine idealized examples of building careers, traveling together, growing a family, sharing joys, and soothing hardships.

In many ways, this is also a fantasy stage because there is so little to lose at this point. The relationship isn't real yet, but it's powerful because our hopes and dreams are real and our desires are intense. In this "honeymoon" stage, our imaginations allow all stories to have happy endings.

The Intimacy Stage

The wall has come down. Relationships at this stage are built on openness. Increased closeness strengthens the bond for future trials.

Eric had always regarded his connection with Tasha as a work friendship. They had been on the same project team for the past year and enjoyed excellent creative chemistry. They often ended up sitting together at outside work functions, catching up on personal stories and current events. They had become workplace "best friends." Eric wasn't sure what to make of the recent discovery of romantic feelings for Tasha. Was it possible she felt the same way about him? The opportunity to consider a different level of connection was an unexpected surprise.

At first, the workplace friendship was simply satisfying. Eric's discovery of romantic feelings surfaced very gradually during the first year of knowing Tasha as a coworker. Until these more intimate feelings of attraction began to make themselves known, he assumed his connection with his colleague was simply a matter of shared interests and natural chemistry.

Intimacy begins as the storybook romance gives way to the realities of life together. Accommodating another person's wishes and priorities into your life requires compromise. As each day moves forward, the awareness of our own needs and desires is blended with an evolving understanding of our partner's frame of reference. Each partner in the romance matures while the relationship changes its shape.

Feelings of trust and desire make the couple eager to dive into life together. The more we know about each other, the deeper the romance. Day by day, issues, challenges, and opportunities are added to the connection. At the same time, increasing closeness is fueled by shared experience. The growing cache of memories makes the couple feel connected. Each interaction creates a touch point for future reference. An argument that ended with an apology and hug becomes a norm for future disagreement. The conversation that routinely follows a night at the movies creates a template for exchanging differences of opinion. The unexpected flat tire on the first road trip becomes a story to be retold and embellished for years to come.

Gradually, the hopes and dreams of Discovery become more real. Both joy and struggle become normal and healthy components of a continuously changing union. The investment made in the Intimacy stage raises the stakes and commits the couple to cope with whatever the future may hold.

Slowly, Eric noticed an attraction that extended beyond cohort teamwork. Physically, intellectually, and emotionally, he began to take a more powerful interest in Tasha. Looking at her wasn't the same. Everything about her now captivated him. Her eye color was a deeper brown than ever before. Her voice was like listening to music. Hearing her description of events made him see the world through fresh eyes. Her self-awareness was refreshing.

Unbeknownst to him, Tasha had developed similar feelings. Looking back, she realized the strength of her attraction to Eric had been brewing for a while. While originally fascinated by his creativity and intellect, she found herself enchanted by his movement. She saw both strength and gentleness in every expression. Tasha wondered how these feelings had stayed hidden for so long because they mesmerized her.

As expected and unexpected events unfold, partners either adapt or choose not to adapt. With each choice, the relationship is redefined. With each successful negotiation, trust grows. As trust gains strength, the foundation for exploration gains support.

The growing sexual tension might have been more visible to strangers than it was to Eric and Tasha. They had been operating in their blind spots for months. Having known each other for over a year, routine exchanges already contained tenderness. Previously casual touch now had new meaning. This was uncharted territory.

Allowing closeness ignites vulnerability. The relationship has not been fully tested. Trust is a safety net for exploration. It provides insulation against risk. The Intimacy stage enables partners to fortify their bond while they learn to manage challenges. By blending another person's needs into your priorities, the resources of the relationship are doubled.

The Adventure Stage

Dare to leverage the foundation. Relationships at this stage are built on exploration. Adventure is the fulfillment of Discovery's hope.

> Amanda enjoyed the elegant home Josh's promotion afforded them. She never dreamed of such a comfortable lifestyle. The new car caught the neighbors' eyes and the exotic vacations made for great conversation over coffee with friends. But Josh's late nights with clients were getting out of control. He was never home.
>
> It seemed the new opportunities had come with a price. Amanda enjoyed the status and perks these changes brought to their family. However, she was growing tired of Josh's late nights with clients.

The momentum of the Discovery and Intimacy stages creates a platform for Adventure. The relationship is now capable of growth that neither partner by themselves could have enjoyed. The act of devotion to another person enables partners to stretch. They're ready to make new commitments, get engaged, get married, have kids, launch careers, and explore the world. Physical, emotional, and intellectual intimacy are enhanced by the exploration of the Adventure stage.

This stage often ushers new sexual discovery along with greater levels of emotional maturity. The learning that arises from sexual trial and error is rooted in the mutuality of need-meeting. As a couple's emotional connection enjoys greater levels of trust, the expression of love with minds and bodies becomes its own language. Partners can now experiment with pleasure and expression in ways that grow the ability to communicate the nuances of their love for each other. Another arena has been built to house the growth of the connection.

Partners are now able to go out on a limb and explore. The relationship has sufficient infrastructure to invite curiosity, pose questions, test ideas, create, invent, experiment, and innovate. The connection is now capable of supporting career change, relocation, further education, having kids, establishing a home, and making financial investments. Together, partners can evaluate their tolerance for risk. Sometimes, both partners easily adapt to their new challenges. Other times, a course correction is needed.

> *At first, Amanda patiently attributed Josh's long hours to the demands of his new role. However, he seemed to be arriving home later and later each night.*

Sometimes, Josh arrived home intoxicated following too many rounds of drinks celebrating the successful closing of some business deal. Without realizing it, the definition of "normal" changed in the household. Amanda and the kids had their life and Josh had his. The splitting of the family unit was insidious. It happened so gradually it wasn't noticeable day-to-day. The abundance of amenities cascading from Josh's earnings was buffering the pain.

The increased tolerance for risk can be a jolt of reality. Some of our dreams are realized while others need to be adjusted. The long-term investment in the growth of the connection creates a relationship we can depend on. We feel grounded and strong. We feel loved and like we have a "partner in crime." They know us and they love us. They support our goals. We can grow as teammates and as individuals. The partnership can now begin capitalizing on differences in the same way it leveraged commonalities in earlier stages.

No matter how close two people become, part of being connected to someone else is the mutual appreciation for what is different. Mutual appreciation requires some space. Closeness has a way of blurring the lines between us. Even in the depths of the greatest intimacy and adventure, our minds, bodies, and spirits are not actually joined as one entity. We always retain a solitary part of ourselves where we can retreat to address the healthy need to refuel.

THE SPACE STAGE

Permit a chance to refuel. Relationships at this stage are built on mutual respect. Healthy distance is safe when intimacy has been established.

After ten years of marriage, Carly no longer felt "in love" with Brian. She wondered if she had even been in love in the first place. The spark was gone. Nearing her fortieth birthday, she began to question whether this was all romance had to offer. Was there an opportunity for a fresh start?

Carly had attempted to reignite the romantic ember with Brian on numerous occasions. It seemed like she was always the one to initiate sex which had become increasingly infrequent. Carly and Brian were best friends and good parents. But were they still in love?

For continuous growth to occur, closeness and distance must find a balance. The changes that arise from stretching the relationship need review. Often, this is best done alone. Solitude has a healing force that informs direction for the future.

Strong partners encourage each other to enjoy life outside of the relationship. The foundation of trust and intimacy makes this safe. It is natural to focus on personal interests and goals. Some needs aren't intended to be met within the relationship. Friends, neighbors, and coworkers may provide stimulation and perspective that lies in the blind spot of the primary interpersonal relationship. Individuals have interests in common with many people in their broader circles. It's not realistic to think that a partner can fulfill every need.

Their intimacy had steadily declined since the kids were born. For nearly a decade, Carly had just endured the frustration, trying to appreciate the wonderful home, friends, and kids that blessed her existence. But now, at this stage of her life, the absence of romance was taking a toll.

The complexity of interpersonal connections creates the need for introspection. Close relationships allow for space whenever they need it. Whether savoring a period of growth or evaluating new circumstances, moving away from the relationship brings clarity. Distance lends perspective when making tough decisions, negotiating disagreements, managing conflicting expectations, weighing other's perceptions, and figuring out how to balance two sets of needs. Maybe the Adventure stage didn't go as planned. Perhaps there's a need to adjust expectations in light of new realities.

> *Beyond the lack of intimacy, daily interactions were mundane and dreary. There was no adventure and the relationship became stale. Each new day was the same as the last. Before having kids, life was fun. There was always an impromptu party in the neighborhood. They took vacations and wandered unfamiliar places with no schedule or agenda. Carly and Brian found humor in every adventure.*
>
> *Lately, though, there wasn't much laughter. They just moved through the business of their days like robots. Carly struggled to imagine the current state of affairs as her future. She wasn't yet sure what to do but knew something had to change. Being so close to the problem made it hard to be objective and make good decisions. Carly had to get some distance from the situation.*

Space also provides a chance to recharge the energy in a relationship. Interactions can become routine and predictable as days turn to weeks and months. Complacency is easily mistaken for neglect when interactions don't seem fresh. The Space stage is as natural as a night's sleep between daily activities. Refueling the emotional bank account enables generosity and altruism.

The Space stage feeds the advancement of the relationship. When partners come back together, they reconnect at a deeper level by virtue of the rest and clarity they have achieved. There's no need to fear being apart. The connection merely becomes better prepared for the next phase of Discovery.

Guiding Principles

Principle #1

Like all living things, relationships evolve in cycles. Without investment, all relationships deteriorate. With investment, relationships grow stronger and more adaptive.

In the absence of attention, living things grow weak. A garden will fade if not watered and weeded. Beyond sustenance, even pets crave contact. As an entity, a human connection requires feeding beyond whatever devotion is paid to each individual. When we feed a relationship, it grows. When we starve it, it gradually loses strength.

In sociological theory, the term *entropy* refers to the way all living things gradually spiral toward their demise. If you never exercise a muscle, it atrophies. When a relationship is neglected, partners fail to thrive. The opposite of entropy is *negentropy*. Living things grow when fed. When you invest in the life of another person, he or she blossoms.

This is a basic recipe for healthy relationships: when you devote your energies to each other, support each other's growth, and adapt to the changes in your circumstances, the connection continuously evolves.

> *Sometimes I joke with my wife of thirty-six years that I have been married six times – to the same person.*
>
> *Our first marriage was when we were 21 years old, starting new jobs, and without kids. Although we were technically adults, we were really a couple of grown-up kids playing house.*
>
> *Our second marriage was defined by the introduction of children and the transition to parental roles. By this time, there was precious cargo on board and our choices had greater consequences.*
>
> *The third marriage transformed when our kids became teenagers. The risks were greater with adolescents in the mix.*
>
> *The fourth marriage evolved after the kids grew up and left home. The two of us needed to recalculate*

our goals and identities as the family's center of attention shifted.

The fifth marriage was when, as young adults, they returned to the home. The family launch pad always prepares for a false start or two.

And now, the sixth marriage is the two of us alone again - but this time as a middle-aged couple rather than a pair of 21-year-olds learning how to play house.

The years roll on and the marriage keeps adapting. One of these days, a seventh marriage will unfold as retirement and grandchildren are introduced to the picture. Perhaps an eighth or ninth marriage will greet us if we are lucky enough to age gracefully into our later years.

Relationship cycles are usually experienced as life stages. Each stage has its own joys and struggles. When you are struggling, it's sometimes hard to see that the transition to the next phase of the cycle may bring resolution. It might be the struggle itself that solves the dilemma. Working together through pleasure and pain, partners grow into each life stage together.

As the relationship moves through its lifespan, new *discoveries* lead to greater intimacy.

 A stronger foundation of *intimacy* supports new adventures.

 Adventure creates growth and requires couples to learn new ways to cope with change.

 Change requires *space* for learning and the lessons are leveraged for another round of discovery.

The cycles continue unless you succumb to the forces of fear or complacency. We all get stuck from time to time. Sometimes, enduring the problem seems easier than tackling the challenge. When you acknowledge and accept the eternal nature of growth, you learn to embrace the change and run with it.

Be ready to invest. Understand your new realities and focus on making them great. Rather than fearing and resisting the next stage, find new ways to enjoy the discovery, intimacy, adventure, and space that unfolds.

Principle #2

Every stage drives the stage opposite to it on the cycle.

© Copyright 2014 Team Clock Institute

Intimacy is not possible without negotiating Space. Discovery is a requirement of Adventure. At any stage of a relationship, partners are always working on the active stage of the cycle and, at the same time, working passively on its opposite stage.

A client once told me she wished she had taken the time to understand some of the fundamental differences she and her fiancé had on sensitive topics such as parenting approach and in-law relations. She said these were topics that got "skimmed over" because they were uncomfortable, and she now regrets not hashing them out. In retrospect, she said, they just assumed everything would work itself out. By avoiding the frustration, they wove unresolved disagreement into the fabric of their relationship. With each passing event, these issues become more deeply rooted and, eventually, experienced as normal day-to-day tensions. In time, the couple stops noticing the symptoms of unsettled matters and just learns to live with the negative emotions that are evoked when controversial topics arise.

In the following chapters, we will take a close look at the subtle dynamics that unfold in each stage of a relationship. We'll examine some pitfalls and see why relationships get stuck. By looking at the struggles of the four couples we met earlier in this chapter, we'll consider how to avoid getting stuck and how to get unstuck when adversity occurs.

Chapter Two
Discovery

Testing the waters and sampling desire: relationships at this stage are built on fun. Discovery lays the groundwork for future adventure.

Trevor's trip to Detroit turned out better than either he or Kiera had expected. They found a nice restaurant near the ballpark and caught up on the conversations that had been started on the phone. Much like their initial date, time spent together flowed naturally. Kiera enjoyed hearing about Trevor's triathlon preparation. Trevor thought he might have convinced Kiera to consider training for a marathon. Kiera and Trevor were both athletes and prided themselves in their commitment to wellness. On their last night together in Detroit, Kiera took Trevor to a small nightclub where a local band was just finishing their second set. They struck up a conversation with the band's guitarist during the break, where Kiera was surprised to *learn of Trevor's guitar collection. He agreed to play for her when she came to Cleveland.*

Trevor looked forward to Kiera's trip to Cleveland later in the summer. Three months was going to be a long time without face-to-face contact. Like their previous separation, Trevor promised to call daily and they both boosted their cell phone contracts to unlimited text plans. Trevor was determined not to lose momentum. The relationship was heating up.

Relationships are fueled by the need for connection. The initial challenge is to negotiate the rules of engagement and find a way to manage differences. Most of us keep our guards up pretty high at the beginning. We've all been hurt before. These early rhythms rest delicately on first impressions. We test each other to see whether our partners will live up to the images we've formed in our minds. With each interaction, a foundation is built that will eventually either succeed or fail to support the tougher challenges the relationship has to offer.

Three months dragged slowly. True to his word, Trevor used nearly every free moment to reach out to Kiera. They indulged the urge to ask questions and share feelings. As if they were compensating for the geographical distance, the pace of the relationship continued to move at a sprint – perhaps too fast. Ki-

era didn't expect to become annoyed with Trevor's constant texting, but it soon became too much. Every time her phone would sound an alert, she braced for another "get to know you" question.

Trevor's constant phone calls were getting under Kiera's skin. She didn't like the reaction she was having. Kiera reached out to the friend who had made the original introduction and confessed the change in her feelings. Her friend immediately noticed the absence of school-girl excitement in Kiera's voice. After hearing her out, Kiera's friend suggested she tell Trevor how she was feeling. She was sure Trevor would understand.

Kiera called right away. Carefully, she explained that while getting to know him had been fun, the constant questions were getting annoying. Trevor became quiet and, after an extended silence, said he understood. The texting slowed over the next few weeks, but Kiera felt like Trevor was pouting. Now, in addition to the constant texting, his neediness seemed to scream immaturity.

Kiera wanted to regain the charm that glowed when they were last together. For his part, Trevor wasn't sure what he had done wrong. He, too, struggled to recapture the bond, but everything he tried seemed to push Kiera away.

This is where the opportunity of Discovery begins. In the first stage of the cycle, partners decide how to invest in each other. The goal is to become attached. Because loss is a common experience, the earliest steps toward closeness are cautious. Plenty of testing is needed to figure out whether the connection is worth the challenge. This phase usually includes some conflict as partners figure out their rules of engagement. After all, if they are going to make a commitment to move forward together, they must forge a common vision for their future and agree on what's most important. As these points get hammered out, every relationship sets its own unique rhythm.

Part of Kiera's confusion was that, physically, Trevor was seriously attractive. She found herself completely absorbed in his good looks. When she was focused on his appearance, his personality quirks seemed to disappear. However, the recently uncovered neediness in Trevor's personality subtracted from his attractiveness.

Trevor found Kiera attractive, as well. But Kiera's feedback made him question where the relationship was headed. It didn't feel good to be criticized and he felt punished for being an attentive boyfriend. He decided it would be best to back off, let some time pass, and try to better understand Kiera's point of view.

Every relationship has its own rules and rhythms. The rules are as unique as the personalities that form the partnership. Paying attention to these nuances builds a gradual foundation as partners test out new behaviors and share more and more of themselves with each other.

Both Kiera and Trevor missed the daily contact. Trevor hesitated to stir anything up for fear of pushing Kiera further away. Kiera wanted more of Trevor, not less. She realized Trevor's ability to open up would be the true test of this new romance. If the two of them could share more than the easy, superficial conversations, they might reclaim the original buzz.

The more Kiera thought about it, the more she realized she hardly knew him. Will he be good with children? How will he react in an emergency? You don't discover these things by texting questions back and forth, indulging sexual urges, or going to baseball games. These are the parts of relationships that become clear over time as you move through situations together. As she considered these discoveries, Kiera's enthusiasm for the relationship began to reignite.

Likewise, Trevor was experiencing his own frustration in trying to get to know Kiera. She wasn't exactly opening up whenever he volleyed his conversation starters. He anxiously awaited a signal from Kiera that it would be safe to resume their discovery of each other. She was a mystery to him and he saw the relationship as a puzzle begging to be solved.

In a subtle way, important questions get answered during this stage of the relationship. How do we handle differences of opinion? Can we stay mature and respectful during conflict? How do we repair the damage when we hurt each other? Intimacy is managed most effectively when interpersonal exchanges ignite struggle and problem-solving. These are the moments when the actual relationship has to live up to the relationship in our imagination. How we work out our differences in theory may bear no resemblance to the way we resolve issues in practice.

It's easy to get stuck in the Discovery stage. The freshness of a new connection fuels a spectrum of positive emotions. Why work when you can play? It's easy to become addicted to the flirtation of the Discovery stage and prevent advancing any further in the cycle.

Some people jump from relationship to relationship because they thrive on the newness and thrill of anticipating the unknown without actually taking any risks. They love the hint of possibility. They savor the fantasy and don't really want a reality check. They don't want to know the real person nor do they wish to be known. They can't progress because they won't open up to another person or allow someone else into their hearts. They don't move forward because they can't accept imperfection in themselves or their partner. Sacrificing the thrill of novelty for the labor of conflict resolution is an undesirable exchange for these individuals.

Take a moment for honest reflection. Answer these questions to know if you might be prone to getting stuck in the Discovery phase.

- What is the average length of your relationships?
- Do you cut people off after one or two dates?
- Are you hesitant to meet someone's family or friends?
- Does conflict make you want to create distance?

Often, this is the moment of truth in the relationship's ability to move forward. Partners must discern whether they are truly incompatible or simply unwilling to try to resolve differences. Intimacy and growth occur only after couples acknowledge and accept the value of struggle. Lasting closeness is dependent on surviving difficulties together, not just celebrating connections. Moving to the next stage involves a conscious decision to lower your guard, get to know your partner, and be willing to be known.

Their phone calls took on a new weight and tone. A blend of caution and risk colored the pace of each sentence. Acknowledging the excitement of the first few months of their time together, Kiera and Trevor both experienced the desire for more depth. Looking back, they realized they hadn't faced any hardships until now. Everything had been focused on fun.

It took them both a while to adjust to the new rhythm. The frequency of phone calls and text messages slowed but the depth and quality was noticeably different. Kiera's trip to Cleveland followed as originally planned but with much less emphasis on dinner and baseball and much more attention to extended conversations. The following day, Kiera joined Trevor at a picnic where she met his family.

Gradually, Kiera began to discover elements of Trevor's background and personality that were more attractive than his athletic body and addictive smile. To her pleasant surprise, she observed how relaxed and natural he was around children at the family picnic. When a few family members started an impromptu jam session, she witnessed Trevor's excellent musicianship. The profile of the man she met on a blind date was filling out.

At the same time, Trevor began to notice the nuances of Kiera's moods. Her pensiveness was as absorbing as her light-heartedness. Rather than trying to cheer her up when she was quiet, he asked what she was thinking. He realized that she just wanted him to listen. He didn't need to fix the problem. Instead of backing off when Kiera was frustrated, Trevor tried to put himself in her position. To his surprise, the intensity of Kiera's negative emotions was just as excit-

ing to him as her positive energy and exuberance.

Getting unstuck requires the willingness to invest in and appreciate the next phase in the cycle. In the Discovery stage, this often means having the discipline to defer some of the excitement until an opportunity has been created to get to know each other at a deeper level. This serves as a preview to aspects of intimacy that eventually become the glue of the connection. Slowly, the walls come down and each partner is portrayed more accurately to the other. The relationship now provides the safety needed to be open and form a bond.

Useful Pain Points

- Going beyond the surface level
- Negotiating mismatched values
- Having tough conversations

Chapter Three
Intimacy

The walls have come down: relationships at this stage are built on openness. Increased closeness strengthens the bond for future trials.

Despite the fact that both Eric and Tasha had experienced a similar rise in romantic feelings after a year of working together, neither had taken the risk to unveil their changing feelings for fear of damaging the quality of the friendship they had formed. Both kept their reactions to themselves until, one day, the intensity of their connection became non-verbally clear during a moment of extended eye contact.

Sharing commonalities brings cohesion to relationships. Yet, dependency requires a blend of nurturance and accountability that fosters comfort and safety. This is hard work. Often, this is the stage where the first impressions break down. We may think our partner has changed when, in fact, he or she just turns out to be different than the person we imagined at the beginning. As our guards gradually lower, closeness is created when our personal needs give way to the chemistry of the bond. The power of the connection tempts partners to unveil more of themselves as each person carefully factors new impressions into their internal profile of the other. The partner we imagined at the beginning evolves to the partner we know now. This image, too, will change.

> *Later, following an after-hours happy hour, a few drinks led to an open conversation where true feelings were unveiled. Both Eric and Tasha were excited by the prospect of sharing closeness at a new level. A year of evolving friendship had created a chance for greater depth.*

Once a decision to share intimacy has been made, trust slowly forms. As partners grow closer, fun, warmth, and interest dominate as they enjoy more togetherness. For many, this stage feels magical. Much of the focus of the connection hinges on what the couple has in common. Like a mirror that offers a favorable reflection, each partner sees the best of themselves in the other person. Excitement grows as both people savor the bond.

> *Eric and Tasha both realized they were voyaging*

into new territory. Now that their feelings had been shared, the impulses were stronger than ever. For both of them, it became difficult to focus on anything else. They quickly grew preoccupied with each other. The situation was moving too fast as other areas of life became neglected. Tasha wanted to slow down but grew more excited whenever they shared closeness. The power of their attraction was having some negative consequences. They needed to figure out the new balance.

At this stage, the relationship pivots on trust. For some, trust starts at zero and has to be earned, action by action. For others, trust is assumed until it is broken. Trust is the consequence of a series of accountability tests where our actions are measured against our words. Each time we pass an accountability test, our connection strengthens. Each time a test fails, our relationship weakens. It's hard to imagine intentionally doing something that subtracts from trust. However, it's possible to neglect trust by failing to realize that every single interaction counts, whether big or small.

When we do what we say we're going to do, we build trust. When we fail to follow through on commitments, we chip away at this foundation. Day by day, we either add to or subtract from the ever-changing cache of trust that defines the foundation of our connection. It builds when we take ownership and deteriorates when neglected. Each exchange provides an opportunity to move trust backward or forward.

Trying to tame their attraction was much more difficult than either of them expected. Tasha's work performance began to suffer to the point where her boss asked her if everything was alright. She dismissed his concern with a smile and some reassurance, but it was now clear that her preoccupation was being telegraphed in the workplace.

Likewise, Eric had begun missing project deadlines for the first time in his career history. His work had become a low priority. Outside of the office, his friends complained that they never saw him anymore. While there was nothing wrong with the magical chemistry of their bond, the amount of time and attention devoted to the relationship had grown out of balance with the other demands of their lives.

The rules of engagement change constantly as relationships evolve so the conflicts and challenges that lie ahead can be managed with flexibility. Among the first of these challenges is the ability to sacrifice the comfort of attachment when the relationship needs to grow and change. Although it is tempting to savor the indulgence of oneness during the trust phase, evolution requires the willingness to give up some security so we can stretch ourselves to new levels. We are strongest as partners when our relationships enable independence.

The Intimacy stage has unique vulnerabilities that can get partners stuck. The biggest risk is opening up, being vulnerable, and then not being accepted by the other person. It's much easier to keep the wall partially up to guard against the prospect of getting hurt. The increased investment in each other has simultaneously raised the risk. Gradually, however, the need to guard our emotions can yield to the choice to embrace the new connection. This has its own hazards.

The lowering of guards and untethered sharing bonds two people as one. As if they were in their own romantic orbit, the reality of the world outside of the relationship becomes blurred. People get stuck when they indulge the desire to stay in their cozy love cocoon and not engage in the world together. Their relationship isolates them from others and becomes an obsession.

Tasha confronted Eric with a challenge. They either had to find a way to rebalance life's priorities, or the relationship would need to be put on hold. Tasha explained that because of the intensity with which she had fallen in love with Eric, she had blindly neglected other important people and commitments. This, she said, was no longer acceptable.

Eric was experiencing his own version of personal, family, social, and occupational neglect. He had lost perspective and had put himself at risk of losing some important people in his life. Although they were not sure how to move forward, it was clear something fundamental needed to change.

Eric and Tasha took a step back and reevaluated their priorities as individuals and as a couple. For a while, they cut back on the amount of time they spent together. They reinvested in their friends, their jobs, and their extended families. Not surprisingly, their time together was more intense and satisfying. Adjusting the volume and pace of contact seemed to put things back in balance. By indulging less in each other, Eric and Tasha somehow ended up with a greater degree of intimacy than when they were urgently trying to capture every moment. As a result, more seemed possible.

Togetherness easily becomes indulgent when pleasure is the reward. It's easy to get stuck when it appears that growth will require sacrificing closeness. Getting unstuck requires willingness to invest in and appreciate the next phase in the cycle. In the Intimacy stage, this often means stepping back and re-evaluating the way the connection consumes your life. In a thriving relationship, this bond is used as a platform from which to launch new growth. Now, the partnership has a foundation that is strong enough to support some exploration in the next phase.

The strength of a connection is cumulative. Each situation creates the opportunity to negotiate new challenges and push the development of new abilities. Whenever a struggle gets resolved, the underpinning of the relationship becomes more secure. The couple adds each resolution to their repertoire of coping strategies and then draws from this experience when a new challenge is confronted.

Useful Pain Points

- Navigating the fear of closeness
- Repairing disrespect
- Earning, sustaining, and growing trust

Chapter Four
Adventure

Building on the foundation: relationships at this stage are built on exploration. Adventure is the fulfillment of discovery.

Josh had fully embraced his new lifestyle. Each day was both exciting and scary. He was making more money than he had ever dreamed of making and, for the first time, was able to give Amanda and the kids the best of everything. The price was also steep.

The foundation of connection creates a platform for exploration. Fueled by growth, differences are illuminated as partners find a way to be independent and together at the same time. In most relationships, this is the first time separateness is woven into the fabric of day-to-day activity. Moving in different directions can either strengthen or weaken the connection. Negotiating how involved or uninvolved a couple is in each other's lives can make or break a relationship.

When intimacy joins adventure, couples are forced to define interdependence. Interdependence is not:

- The power differential found in pure dependence.
- The untethered freedom of complete independence.
- The pathological neediness of co-dependence.

Interdependence means finding a way to dovetail two lives in a way that allows both closeness and distance. Each partner is empowered to feel alone when the couple is together and joined when they are apart.

Just how much overlap the couple selects is as unique as the chemistry of their connection. However, the balance has to be negotiated. Ultimately, interdependence strikes the delicate balance between being secure enough to function outside of the relationship and vulnerable enough to engage in a committed connection. Often, this takes a bit of trial and error.

Josh never left the office before 8:00 p.m. and, on many nights, his boss stopped him on his way out to join him for drinks with new clients. One thing led to another, and before Josh knew it - it was often after midnight.

Sometimes closeness demands distance. Consider the

typical reaction to receiving a hug that lasts too long – the urge to push away is normal. In contrast to the togetherness of the previous stage, all relationships eventually crave some individuality. While it feels good to be joined as one, healthy relationships create enough space for individual exploration and creativity. Strong connections are based on more than togetherness. They also rely on an appreciation of differences. The payoff for the effort expended during the Discovery and Intimacy stages is the safety to explore new experiences with the confidence that the relationship will adapt to whatever changes happen to unfold. The prospect that this exploration will have a positive outcome, however, is not guaranteed.

> *Amanda was concerned about Josh's safety and grew increasingly angry when these occasional occurrences started to happen more regularly. When Josh failed to call or didn't respond to texts, Amanda's worry about his well-being changed to frustration about his constant absence and unavailability to the family. Their arguments grew more intense and would quickly spiral downward to name-calling and mud-slinging. This was not the life she ever imagined having, and all the amenities in the world wouldn't matter if something awful happened to their family.*

Growing relationships move forward with permission to

experiment. Many of the differences discovered in the early stages of the connection are leveraged to create new possibilities for the couple. While sometimes scary, the excitement that accompanies creativity fuels new energy in the relationship.

Josh was initially angry when Amanda finally spoke after three days of the silent treatment. By the time Amanda found enough time and space to gain some clarity, Josh anticipated the argument and was well prepared to shoot down her complaints with examples of the benefits the family enjoyed.

By sacrificing some of the comfort of the previous stage, couples generate opportunities for adventure. Stretching limits and inviting new journeys doesn't always work out smoothly. Mistakes are made. The lessons of struggle become the drivers of growth.

For Amanda, it wasn't about the benefits. The wealth the couple was now enjoying was not an acceptable trade-off for the changes that had happened in their relationship. She felt she had lost her husband and their children had lost their father. The big house had become a lonely place.

The inevitable consequence of growth is change. Monitoring the overall wellness of the relationship during this stage is essential. If the norms and values that created the foundation of the connection are lost, the relationship can become vulnerable. On the other hand, attention to the rules of engagement that originally defined the relationship can serve as an anchor of stabilization when waters get rough.

Heated arguments filled most of their limited time together. The tension spilled over to the kids as teachers reported lack of focus and peer conflicts in the classroom. They were clearly distracted. This was the tipping point. It was one thing to have conflict in the marriage. It was another to cause distress for their children.

The ability to flow with the ups and downs and embrace the full spectrum of daily life together requires courage. When the earlier stages of the relationship have been defined by a sustained emotional high, any significant change feels like catastrophe. The circumstances no longer bear any resemblance to the rhythm that shaped the stages of Discovery and Intimacy. Each phase of life together brings a new adventure with demands for coping skills that were never before needed. The struggle itself produces new relationship competencies.

At first, Josh minimized the impact of his absence on the kids' struggles. He suggested they were just going through a stage. However, Amanda saw a direct cause-and-effect correlation between Josh's intense focus outside of the home and their children's difficulties. Whether sporting events or musical performances, the kids now regularly asked why daddy wasn't there. Deep down, Josh knew she was right. But on the outside, he held his ground.

Many couples get stuck in the Adventure stage. The stakes are much higher than ever before, and the higher intensity requires a new level of adaptability. Growth rarely happens on a straight-line trajectory. New abilities advance when insight provides clarity, and coping retreats when the pain of growth becomes hard to endure. Both partners govern the pace of growth. Couples can forge ahead or take a break as they consider each other's feedback. Changes get negotiated and the relationship evolves.

It was abundantly clear to Amanda that the cost of the changes that had occurred in their lives was too great to continue on this path. She invited Josh to consider setting better boundaries at work. Perhaps they would still have enough income to support their lifestyle while providing more reasonable hours and time with Amanda and the kids. Josh predicted ca-

reer suicide. He was frustrated by Amanda's lack of appreciation for what happens to men at his stage of life when they decline career advancement. The opportunities stop coming. You get labeled. Once you decline late nights and travel, they find a new young up-and-comer who's willing to sacrifice everything for a chance to advance.

Embarking on an adventure means willingness to make mistakes and use those missteps to inform new possibilities. Experiments, by their nature, are designed to prove the wisdom of an idea. Failed experiments are often gifts. They illuminate new paths when couples find themselves stuck. Getting unstuck requires an appreciation for the next phase in the cycle.

Amanda did her best to understand this fear, but held firm that the health and wellness of their marriage and family was a higher priority. She delivered the ultimatum. It was one or the other. Josh had to make a decision. In time, he relented. When he stepped back and looked at the big picture, it grew clear that he had not expanded his ability to manage his responsibilities – he had just taken hours from home and reallocated them to work. He was losing his wife and kids while spending energy defending his choices. True growth would mean finding a way to enhance his family and his career, not one at the expense of the other.

In the Adventure stage, this often means acknowledging the need for time and space. Because the challenges are new, the problem needs additional study and consideration. Since adventure consumes energy, partners need a chance to recharge their batteries. Eventually, time and space bring clarity as the strength of the relationship built in its earlier stages comes to the aid of the connection. Healthy couples thank their mistakes and capitalize on the lessons arising from the choice to have stretched themselves. The pain, in the end, is useful.

The change was an adjustment for everyone. Josh was unable to pull in quite as much money as the family had become accustomed to. Once he began declining late night business outings, the invitations became less frequent. Dinner conversations and bedtime rituals had to be altered to welcome Josh back into the rhythm and flow of the household. Some of the tension that had built up between Josh and Amanda occasionally resurfaced when either of them was tired or overwhelmed. Overall, though, the family togetherness they came so close to losing was slowly rebuilt. Even with a less ambitious career, there were enough financial and emotional resources to have a good life and a close family.

The labor of the earlier stages now pays off. If the testing, conflict, and accountability aren't handled successfully in the Discovery and Intimacy phases, the Adventure stage is doomed. When managed effectively, all prior struggles strengthen the foundation by creating an archive of experience. The lessons learned at each pain point are delivered to the next stage of growth.

Useful Pain Points

- Challenging the status quo
- Finding value in differences
- Devoting time and resources to untested ideas

Chapter Five
Space

A chance to refuel: relationships at this stage are built on mutual respect. Healthy distance is safe if intimacy has been established.

Carly and Brian were probably equally guilty of neglecting the relationship. They both knew their intimacy had suffered ever since the children were born. While they were great friends, romance had disappeared in their relationship. Even the little things had disappeared. They rarely chose to spend time together whenever the kids were occupied outside of the house, preferring to go in separate directions.

Evolution alters people and their circumstances. It forces us to move with the flow of change. Adapting with flexibility takes poise. For most of us, our coping skills are at their best under normal conditions. Under stressful conditions, however, our coping skills tend to break down. We regress. We fall back to the less mature reactions that had accompanied previous significant or traumatic events in our lives. At best, trying to stay nimble and agile under tough circumstances depletes energy. It's exhausting.

The lack of physical intimacy was the most glaring problem, but the less obvious symptoms were pervasive. Brian never surprised Carly with flowers anymore, and Carly lost motivation to surprise Brian with a warm batch of his favorite chocolate chip cookies like she did when they were first married. The marriage had suffered from neglect.

When Carly finally voiced her displeasure, she did her best to take ownership of her share of the responsibility but blamed Brian for the absence of any spark in their physical relationship. After a long and awkward conversation, Brian acknowledged his role in the problem and agreed to be more attentive.

Almost immediately, he became more focused on Carly's needs by commenting on her attractiveness, initiating hugs, sitting next to her to watch one of her TV shows, and going to bed at the same time as she did. At first, Carly was optimistic that Brian had gotten the message, and she, too, began paying more attention to him. However, Brian's efforts to be more romantic were short-lived, and he soon returned to his previous inattentive style. Carly was frustrated. She felt teased by the return of his attention and now, once again, had lost her partner.

Change requires partners to move away from established patterns. One way or another, the nature of the relationship evolves. The new circumstances require different skills and behaviors than were needed before. When partners give each other the gift of independence, they also accept the loss that comes from the changes they have created. Eventually, the relationship will need to reinvest in the new circumstances. Before this can occur, the partners need to acknowledge and mourn what has been lost.

Over the course of a long relationship, the ground rules get redefined numerous times. Couples invest in different priorities. They are accountable for new responsibilities. The stakes are raised when kids are added to the picture. Dealing with change gets more difficult. Constant adjustment to new conditions is the only way to thrive. As much as either partner may want things to stay the same, they can't.

For weeks, Carly weighed the pros and cons of divorcing. There would be so many changes and so many losses. Of course, the future would be unknown, but the more she thought about it - the harder it was to imagine living the second half of her adult life without intimacy.

Brian never dreamed Carly would walk away. He had come from a family history where divorce would never be a consideration. You always find a way to work things out. So, it came as a surprise to Brian when Carly eventually told him she wanted to separate.

Change and loss are inevitable aspects of all relationships. Reacting to disappointment and adversity with agility is difficult. For most of us, significant change drains our energy. We become depleted. Depletion makes it harder to invest energy in working on the relationship. Slowing down helps us make the time needed for relationships to reflect, react, and adjust.

Sometimes it appears a partner is resisting change when they are really just adapting at a slower pace. Everyone's pace for dealing with loss is unique to his or her history and circumstances. Often, resistance provides a protective function by preventing change from happening so fast that it causes additional damage.

Brian urged Carly to reconsider. He accused her of holding on to unrealistic "fairy tale" expectations. The space between them widened. The couple painfully negotiated a transition. After a few contentious exchanges, they hired lawyers and divided assets. Yet, their long-standing friendship served as a foundation for a largely collaborative process. Carly located a new place to live close enough to the family home that the kids could navigate between the two houses with ease. Once all of the arrangements had been made and the family had settled into their new lifestyles, Carly filed for divorce.

Loss is new territory for most relationships. Whether the change is positive or negative and whether it is within or beyond your control, a sense of grief settles in when you come face to face with the enormity of the change that has happened in your life. Regardless of your past experience with loss, each one is unique as it reflects the nuances of that particular connection. For most of us, absence is more noticeable than presence. It isn't until something is gone that we realize how much we miss it. Perhaps the way it used to be can never be recaptured. Maybe the connection needs to get redefined to accommodate the new realities in both partners' lives.

About six months after Carly filed for divorce, a court date was scheduled to finalize the process. Throughout that time, the couple negotiated a litany of details. For the most part, their exchanges were amicable. Often, they arranged babysitters and met in a public place to minimize the kids' exposure to adult details.

About a week before the court date, the couple went out for dinner to hammer out a few remaining items. As the conversation unfolded, they both began to wonder out loud whether divorcing was a mistake. Carly wondered to herself whether she could really let Brian go. Brian noticed Carly's attractiveness and chastised himself for taking her beauty for granted. In the months since separating, they had gotten along better than ever before. Carly and Brian came to realize it was a form of closeness and intimacy they were exchanging as they navigated their delicate situation. They missed each other. The near reality of the loss had served as a wake-up call.

Finding the time to take stock of changes allows energy to be recouped. As partners position themselves to address their new circumstances, a new expenditure of energy will be required. The transition from distancing, separation, and loss into a renewed phase of discovery will provide an influx of new energy for the couple. Thus, the cycle of opportunities begins anew.

After dismissing the divorce, Carly and Brian found a professional counselor to assist them in re-establishing their relationship. They realized the foundation they had built over the past ten years was a great starting point but they would need to push themselves and each other to evolve as a couple. To successfully reboot the relationship, they were going to need some help and guidance along the way. They needed to accept the reality that things would never be the same with the hope that they could grow into a new and exciting next chapter of their lives together.

Like no other phase of the relationship cycle, the Space stage is when couples are most vulnerable to getting stuck or giving up. A fight or disagreement is sometimes just the emotional need to be alone for a while as clarity about direction works its way to awareness. If the relationship isn't firmly rooted in openness and trust established in the Intimacy stage, the dramatic nature of change that arises from the Adventure stage can break the bond.

Some couples can travel through an adventure together, but they don't have what it takes to manage all the demands of sharing a lifetime together. Not all relationships are meant to stay together. Sometimes it can't be fixed. There may be a strong friendship, but there might not be enough of a base of shared values to build their life on. The Space phase sometimes functions as permission to split up. Also, some people actually like to get stuck in this stage. They enjoy holding grudges, seeing themselves as a victim, and never admitting they're wrong. They are always unhappy, no matter whom their partner is.

Eventually, partners have to question whether the relationship has become a vehicle to house their displeasure — whether they're using each other to work out bigger core issues in their lives. Ideally, the Space stage provides enough distance and objectivity to diagnose sources of struggle and set goals for the couple's next phase of work. At this point of the relationship's growth, couples aren't starting over. They're simply renewing the long term commitment to keep moving through the cycles together and improving the product rather than repeating old patterns.

In the strongest relationships, time and space provide the fuel and clarity to propel the relationship past the crisis into the next opportunity for discovery. Once the partners come back together and share the lessons unveiled by the temporary distance, a chance to refocus on the new circumstances of the relationship unfolds.

It was like starting over. They agreed to move forward as if everything were open to negotiation. At the base of their new challenge was a recently discovered, deeply rooted love for each other — not quite a romantic glow, but a solid friendship and foundation of respect. Recognizing they were pretty young when they first began dating, Carly and Brian realized they had rushed through many of the essential elements of getting to know each other.

While not completely possible after a decade of living together, they committed to what they affectionate-

ly called a "do-over." At first, it seemed a bit artificial when they would invite conversation about the day's activities. The dialogue was initially a little forced. In time, these exchanges took on a rhythm, and both Brian and Carly began to look forward to their evening review sessions.

These conversations became opportunities to express feelings and practice better listening skills. Both Carly and Brian began to feel like their partner genuinely cared about their lives. Simply taking an interest in the other person's needs seemed to repair the bond that had once appeared broken.

Getting unstuck requires willingness to invest in and appreciate the next phase in the cycle. In the Space stage, this often means a willingness to take a look at the foundation of the relationship and reconsider the bonds that hold the connection together. For some couples, this is a clean slate. By acknowledging what has changed and inviting a fresh look, the relationship is given a chance to evolve with all new strengths and coping skills.

Useful Pain Points

- Letting go of old wounds
- Staying poised and nimble during adversity
- Embracing new circumstances

Chapter Six

Moving Relationships Forward

Relationships get stuck all the time. Getting unstuck requires willingness to invest in and appreciate the next phase in the cycle. The challenge is to identify where you are in the cycle and what opportunities are around the corner. Both partners must be willing to move into the next phase together. Pay attention to your stuck points. They contain the hints for what to do next.

In professional circles, clinicians seek to learn the purpose of a symptom. The symptom (e.g. frustration, complacency, apprehension, depletion) is the voice of opportunity. The therapist is trained to ask the question, "What would need to be true about my client's circumstances to make his or her choices make sense?" "What purpose is the struggle playing in the person's life?" Once you understand the benefit the challenge serves, you can design a treatment plan to alleviate the discomfort. This leaves the clinical professional with two avenues: make the symptom go away or dive into the deeper task of addressing its cause. Even though it provides temporary relief, making the symptom go away stifles the voice of opportunity.

A challenge becomes an opportunity when overcoming it leads us to clarity and growth. Struggle helps us when it spurs the development of new coping abilities. Ignoring or self-medicating emotional pain prevents this opportunity from being realized. Of course, it makes you feel better in the short term. In the long run, though, the problem just sinks its roots more deeply into the relationship. Eventually, the problematic themes need to rise again in new sets of similar circumstances.

Relationship challenges happen in predictable ways during the Discovery phase. Sometimes couples have difficulty managing conflict. Other times they just can't come to an agreement about their future. Likewise, there are typical struggles in the Intimacy phase of the cycle. Sometimes partners don't follow through with commitments. Other times they say or do things that hurt each other. In the Adventure phase, relationships tend to stumble on issues that become obstacles to growth. Some people resist change instinctively. Other people move so far ahead of their partners that they forget to seek input. Of course, the Space phase also has predictable challenges. During a loss, most of us feel tired and unmotivated. It's natural to experience pessimism and a lack of hope.

Let's look at the most typical ways people struggle in relationships. We will consider **ten common challenges**

of relationships: *norms, alignment, conflict, personal connection, respect, accountability, risk, leveraging differences, mourning, and refocusing.* With each example, we will examine the challenge, follow it to its purpose, discuss how struggles help us grow, and consider what these opportunities invite us to do.

CHALLENGES OF THE DISCOVERY STAGE

Challenge #1: Norms

Lisa was an extrovert and Barry was an introvert. In fact, Lisa came from a family of outgoing siblings who filled every weekend with activities. Barry grew up in a family where it was more common to spend a Friday night reading quietly or working alone on a project. For Barry's family, solitude was rejuvenating. In the earliest years of Barry and Lisa's relationship, the anticipation of the weekend caused discomfort as each partner began to dread the other's plans.

Strong relationships have clear agreement on the rules, boundaries, and behaviors that guide day-to-day interactions. Most couples don't sit down and formally set their ground rules. Usually, getting clear about expectations arises from the realization that something is not working. Discomfort can linger until one of the partners discovers the need to clarify a difference. Sometimes, there are unresolved feelings that have settled in and become normalized. It might then dawn on the couple that they don't want an undesirable pattern of interchange to become normal. Everyone has a few old wounds that haven't totally healed, and interpersonal closeness is an easy way to activate them. The goal is to walk into a new relationship with old issues as resolved as possible.

The job of building a foundation of relationship norms is labor intensive. Unless both participants are ready to undertake the challenge, their energy will be steered toward perpetuating old ways rather than refocusing on the new circumstances. Some norms are naturally created and others require intention. Not all of the norms we fall into are helpful. It depends on whether they support or impede productive exchange.

Both partners have to be willing to step back from their own perspectives and consider what ground rules might help the relationship be more effective. Maybe they agree to never go to bed mad and commit to resolving disagreements before each day ends. Perhaps they protect weekends as "sacred" as a way to honor the importance of dedicated time together. Some couples have a "no interrupting" rule to encourage more active listening. Whatever the norms, they are designed to build structure around the wellness of the relationship.

> *Lisa's solution was to develop a social network of friends outside of the marriage. Although Barry had no desire to join Lisa in her weekend activities, he grew jealous of her new friends. When Barry expressed feeling left out of her new world, Lisa was unsympathetic. As far as she was concerned, he was free to join her. Over time, Lisa and Barry developed separate lives. Although they remained married, there was little new investment in a common future.*

Not every couple enjoys success negotiating norms. When they don't, they deliver a lack of resolution to the future of the relationship. For some partners, the "devil you know" is better than the "devil you don't know." The discomfort associated with altering old patterns is harder to imagine than tolerating a pain you're already enduring.

For some couples, the element of maintaining a long-distance relationship adds another layer of complication. Physical proximity often forces a couple to set boundaries and expectations. Partners have to find a way to achieve separateness when they're together. When the connection also faces the challenge of geographical distance, partners need to find a way to achieve closeness when they're apart.

> *Lisa's and Barry's marriage began to resemble a long-distance relationship. Each of their families communicated concern for the health of their relationship. This is not what either of them ever wanted. However, neither of them had anticipated the consequence of having such different sources of social energy. After considerable discussion, they agreed to experiment with each other's preference. Lisa agreed to spend one weekend night each month at home with Barry simply being together. Likewise, Barry agreed to join Lisa and her friends going into the city once a month to try out a new restaurant. It was a small compromise, but it respected each of their preferences and reestablished a baseline of togetherness.*

In time, the struggles preventing the establishment of norms get resolved as people experience the consequences of their choices, seek support from friends and family, and take action in search of resolution. With a fresh start, a new connection has a chance to define its rhythms and routines. Let this unfold. Over time, day-to-day interactions reinforce a commitment to relationship wellness.

Rhythms and routines provide anchors during times of change. Conversations that feed the quest toward healthy norms start with key questions:

- How do we wish to be treated? How can we make kindness and civility a normal way of interacting?
- What are the basic ground rules of our relationship (e.g. address issues as they arise, apologize and make amends, take ownership of mistakes, etc.)?

By addressing some of these questions, Lisa and Barry might form a deeper understanding of their distinct personalities and family histories. Perhaps there is a rhythm and structure in their relationship that might meet both of their needs.

Challenge #2: Alignment

Beth and Jeffrey had been together for five years. Everyone assumed it would be forever, and they often fielded questions from friends and relatives about when they would tie the knot. Jeffrey's family loved Beth and often said she was the best thing that ever happened to him. Beth's family was getting used to Jeffrey. He was a little more free spirited than they were, and his outrageousness would sometimes make them uncomfortable. Regardless, he was kind, funny, and willing to do anything for anybody.

Effective partnerships enjoy clear agreement on roles, responsibilities, and direction. When people struggle with alignment, it's often because they have significant differences in key areas. Perhaps they have dissimilar morals and values. Maybe they have diverse views on religion, politics, or parenting style.

Despite the longevity of their relationship, Beth harbored doubts about a long-term commitment. At 30, she wasn't sure she was ever going to find someone with the chemistry they shared. They found each other attractive and consistently had fun together. They had become good friends and shared a growing collection of memories. However, some important elements of successful relationships seemed missing.

Simply, their values were different. Beth put a lot of stock in the importance of being independent, self-sufficient, and dependable. Jeffrey would agree that these things were important, but his lifestyle choices did not support his words. He spent money freely without much concern for long-term plans. He fell behind on bills and would fail to follow through on commitments. He was often late and, on a few occasions, didn't manage to show up for a date. Jeffrey forgot most birthdays and anniversaries and would scramble to grab a card and a bouquet of flowers at the grocery store on the way home from work on Valentine's Day.

Whatever the differences, finding alignment requires a blend of open communication, understanding, negotiation, tolerance, and acceptance. Depending on the couple's commitment to embracing differences as strengths, disagreements either become irritants that support separateness or enrichments that support togetherness.

The mismatch in their values and common courtesies had become predictable and normal. Everyone joked about it. To Beth, it was no longer funny. Jeffrey's charm had begun to wear thin. She felt like she was holding the relationship together by herself. She expressed to her closest friends that dating Jeffrey was like parenting a child. Beth's mother tried to reassure her that Jeffrey would eventually "grow up," but Beth could hear the doubt in her mother's voice.

Value alignment grows in importance when partners are considering a long-term commitment. If you are "just dating," it's easy to dismiss these chasms as harmless idiosyncrasies. As soon as you begin considering the long-term implications of these foibles, they become fundamental elements of the relationship's foundation. They transform from quirks to character traits.

Beth had attempted to confront Jeffrey with her concerns on many occasions. She had employed a variety of strategies ranging from assisting him with finances to ultimatums. Usually, Jeffrey would become more responsible for a week or two, and then everything would slip back to its original status. It seemed like the only way he would be able to sustain any change would be if she stayed on top of him constantly. This was not the kind of relationship she wanted to have. Beth was not willing to make a long-term commitment with someone for whom she'd become a caretaker nor was she willing to inherit the consequences of his irresponsibility into her future.

Jeffrey would need to decide whether Beth was important enough to him to undertake a transformation. In one final plea, Beth laid it on the line. The only conditions under which she would ever consider moving forward with Jeffrey included a commitment from him to make fundamental changes. Even though Beth entered this conversation with a level of seriousness she believed would serve as a wake-up call, Jeffrey's reaction was no different than any of the previous conversations. He acknowledged her concerns and quickly tried to lighten the situation with charm and humor.

He totally underestimated Beth's conviction. Needless to say, nothing changed.

Sometimes, alignment takes the form of agreeing to disagree. This is easiest when the difference is a preference, an opinion, or a taste. However, when the disagreement is rooted deeply in values or intractable habits, it's hard for couples to align. When the lack of alignment is deeply rooted, it's more likely to remain an irritant as the relationship moves forward. Asking someone to grow up and be more mature is fair. Asking another person to change the basic structure of their character is a tenuous way to start a relationship.

Beth took the time to weigh her circumstances and engaged a few close friends, family, and trusted colleagues in a careful review of her options. Once she gained a sense of clarity in her direction, she invited Jeffrey over for dinner for the purpose of bringing the relationship to an end. Jeffrey could tell from the tone of her voice on the phone that something was wrong. He asked her to reveal the subject of her concern, but Beth insisted that the discussion happen face-to-face. She hung up the phone and awaited Jeffrey's arrival.

Jeffrey was late. As usual, he had a litany of excuses for his tardiness. Every imaginable obstacle had jumped in front of his path. Beth was calm and deter-

mined in her demeanor. She respectfully reviewed the history and source of her frustration and recounted the numerous attempts the two of them had made to find resolution. When Jeffrey realized that Beth was breaking up with him, he urgently promised to change. He promised to become everything she wanted him to be if she would just give him one last chance. Unfortunately, this was the last "last chance."

After five years of weaving families and friends together, dismantling the relationship was delicate. Beth did her best to carry herself in a fashion that minimized awkwardness whenever they were brought together in social situations. She fended off urges to allow the fun rhythms of their natural chemistry to be revived. She remained true to her decision. Jeffrey spent some time licking his wounds. First and foremost, he had been dumped. It took him a while to accept the feedback from his inner circle of friends that he had let a wonderful partner slip away.

Some differences are unresolvable. Alignment isn't always possible. On the other hand, the power of discovery also includes an invitation to adapt. When respected, opposites often attract. Differences strengthen a relationship when they are acknowledged and appreciated. At best, they create a balance of variety that helps the relationship stretch in new directions.

Appreciate the value of diversity while identifying the common themes that bring you together. Conversations that strengthen alignment start with key questions:

- What are our common and different views on religion, politics, parenting, extended family relationships, friends?
- How do we see the role of money in our lives? What are our short-term and long-term financial priorities?
- What are our common and different interests (e.g., use of free time, hobbies, arts, sports, current events)?

Beth turned the corner. She recommitted herself to the areas of her life that best supported her health including her career, social network, community activities, and general wellness. Likewise, Jeffrey was forced to rethink his choices. Perhaps this was just a maturity issue rather than an indictment of his character. The future was unclear for both Beth and Jeffrey. It was possible they would end up alone. Maybe they would each find someone else. Perhaps their lives would find a reason to intersect again under different conditions. In any case, they would both need to reinvest in the discovery of their new circumstances.

Challenge #3: Conflict

Erin and Michael never imagined the family battles that would ensue when they began planning their wedding. Erin was fully aware of the differences in their family backgrounds. Financial, religious, moral, and political disagreements always managed to add tension to the conversation during family gatherings. Fortunately, Erin and Michael had found a way to use these differences as strengths in their relationship. They viewed the diversity as a rich palette that added color and tone to their conversations.

However, the wedding planning required a greater amount of family interaction. Michael's mom envisioned a far more traditional ceremony than Erin had in mind. Whenever the women attempted to hammer out their differences, the exchange became personal and hurtful.

Healthy relationships value and engage in productive, respectful conflict. When people mismanage conflict, an opportunity to enjoy the benefits of differences has been lost. The art of conflict is rooted in fairness and respect. When partners become disrespectful of each other's viewpoints, the goal of the exchange is to protect your own interests rather than to seek understanding or compromise. In extreme situations, a triangle forms between the relationship partners and some other entity.

Whenever a third element is added to the relationship, the core dyad must stay anchored as the primary connection or the third element will wield the most power. In the graphic below, the strengths of the primary couple is transferred to the mother-son alliance. The primary romance is sacrificed and compromised.

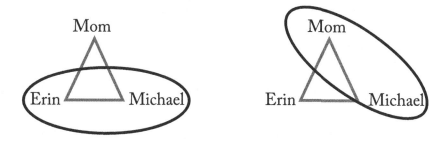

It's easy to see how conflict ceases to be a negotiation between two people when a third-party influence is introduced, such as in-laws, friends, extra-marital affairs, addictions, financial pressures, and work demands. In these examples, the third party governs the priorities of the negotiation.

Eventually, Michael stepped in. He attempted to navigate the conflict between his fiancé and his mother to no avail. His mother was unwilling to budge, and Erin began to wonder whether her mother-in-law would become a wedge in future marital decisions. This was more than she had bargained for.

Healthy conflict requires clear rules and solid problem-solving techniques. First, both parties should be calm and clear minded. Second, the discussion can only remain productive if both people are committed to respectful interaction. Name calling, hitting below the belt, and dredging up old business not only prevents the conversation from moving forward but increases the damage being caused to your partner and yourself.

Once the ground rules are in place, employ a series of simple problem-solving steps:

1. Define the problem specifically and discuss the impact on each person.
2. Brainstorm all possible solutions with respect for differences.
3. Weigh the pros and cons of each option objectively.
4. Act on what appears to be the best choice.
5. Learn from your decision and make changes if necessary.

Stay on task, check understanding, clarify misunderstandings, and summarize learning. Conversations that lead to respectful and productive conflict start with key questions:

- How do I feel when my partner is angry or disappointed in me?
- What are our greatest areas of disagreement in this relationship?

Erin and Michael will need to elevate their conflict management style to prevent family politics from ruining their wedding. More importantly, the failure to set clear boundaries in the beginning could have lasting consequences for the future of the relationship. Michael will need to decide whether he is married to Erin or his mother.

In a successful Discovery stage, couples establish clear relationship norms, see a common direction for the future, and learn to appreciate and resolve their differences.

Challenges of the Intimacy Stage

Challenge #4: Personal Connection

David and Rachel had been dating casually for over a year. The relationship was gradually becoming more serious, and they had begun having conversations about a commitment to a longer-term arrangement. The transition from dating to talking about commitment had implications neither of them had considered. For instance, David wondered whether he should tell Rachel about his arrest for marijuana possession during his college years. He had a criminal record, and even though many years had passed, it could have implications for his career path.

Relationships that evolve positively are characterized by open, candid interactions. When people struggle with personal connection, they are often protecting themselves from feeling vulnerable. It's natural to fear intimacy when growing close to someone.

What if you reveal a part of yourself that your partner

finds undesirable? What might your partner think of you if he or she knew your secrets?

We all maintain some level of guardedness between what we think and feel internally and what we let the outside world see. Lowering that guard makes us vulnerable to misunderstanding. But it also opens up the possibility for closeness and connection that feeds our hearts with goodness and hope for the future. Despite the prospect of attachment, many of us hold back.

> *Rachel wondered whether she should reveal the brief psychiatric hospitalization that occurred following a suicide gesture after a night of drinking with friends during her adolescence. Only her family and a few close friends were aware of this secret. She wondered whether David would think differently about her if he knew about this history and that she still sometimes struggles with depression.*

Intimacy usually overrides secrets and trauma histories. Most sensitive information is better off shared when a couple decides to indulge their attachment and commit to a longer term future. When you allow yourself to be vulnerable in the presence of another person, you find out quickly about his or her ability to love unconditionally. When you learn a sensitive piece of information from someone for whom you care, you are given the gift of an opportunity to help him or her heal and grow within the safety of your understanding and acceptance.

Personal connection takes many forms. Partners share bodies, thoughts, feelings, and dreams. Conversations that lead to greater attachment and intimacy start with key questions:

- In what realm do we most often experience our connection with each other (physical, emotional, intellectual, social, cultural, spiritual)?
- What aspects of my partner do I find most compelling and endearing?

David and Rachel will eventually learn that there is more to intimacy than sharing secrets and personal histories. Delving into these questions will help them discover the subtle qualities they appreciate about each other, including the richness and variety of their pasts.

Challenge #5: Respect

When Tom and Barbara met, they shared their family histories with each other. Most of these exchanges were presented in the form of stories that had shaped their childhood and adolescent years. Some of these stories, however, were personal and sensitive. When Barbara revealed the history of her mother's extramarital affair, she never dreamed it would end up being recounted in a social gathering of their college friends.

Partners in strong relationships deliver a healthy sense of unconditional positive regard. When people struggle with respect, they often either hurt their partner by saying or doing something degrading or they violate a level of personal privacy or confidentiality. These are the most damaging breaches in relationships. When we choose to make ourselves vulnerable to another person, we are owed the assurance that our vulnerability won't be violated. We are entitled to the confidence that our partners won't say or do hurtful things.

Relationships that tolerate disrespect, belittlement, degradation, meanness, or cruelty are designed to make one person feel stronger at the expense of making another person feel weaker. An imbalance is woven into the fabric of the connection. Relationships that permit the violation of privacy are, by design, not safe. I can't share something intimate with you if I fear it will be made public. There must be matters that stay strictly between the two of us.

Although she didn't show her anger at the moment, Barbara was furious when she overheard Tom revealing the sensitive details of one of the most painful periods of her life. She felt like her privacy was not important in his eyes. Tom's obliviousness to this violation was further evidence that he was unaware of the sensitivity of the breach.

Respect is strengthened or weakened with every interaction. Partners seeking to reinforce their trust with a foundation of respect must exercise daily stewardship over the most sensitive aspects of their sharing. Beyond the obvious avoidance of hurtful words and actions, both people possess a responsibility for protecting matters that are sacred in their connection with each other.

Learn to be clear about what you want shared. Use discretion. Often, there's no need to share every last detail of everything that is sensitive. We all need to strike a balance that both invites a partner to partake in our lives while protecting what's private, as well.

The closer it is to your heart, the more it needs to be safeguarded. If you stumble and commit some kind of breach, take ownership, apologize, and prove the integrity of your intent by changing your behavior in the future. This is the essence of respect in a relationship.

There is no need for hidden agendas, ulterior motives, or manipulation when a relationship is rooted in mutual respect. Conversations that support respect in a relationship start with key questions:

- How would I most like to be treated during sensitive times?
- How can I best show you that I appreciate your feelings and will treat them considerately?

Tom and Barbara will need to learn to protect the boundaries of their relationship by defining what is sacred. Even though Tom's actions were not intended to hurt Barbara, they did. The experience of disrespect created an interpersonal crisis in their relationship and showed them that every interaction has meaning and consequences. Moving forward with new awareness will be a gift to future delicate moments when respect will more likely prevail.

Challenge #6: Accountability

Mark and Susan had been married for ten years and had three children. Outwardly, they appeared to have the perfect family. Mark coached his son's baseball team, and Susan volunteered for numerous charity events in the community. They had many friends and hosted many gatherings in their home.

What their friends and family didn't know was that their physical intimacy had been on the decline since the birth of their first child. Occasional awkward sex-

ual encounters had kept the romantic embers glowing at a low level for a while and had even produced two other children. But since the birth of the third child, they had been sleeping in separate bedrooms.

Smaller breaches of accountability are often repaired by taking responsibility, apologizing, and committing to different behavior in the future. These are the course corrections of relationships. Large breaches of trust undermine the foundation of a relationship. Repairing this level of damage must be done carefully and gradually. Building back trust happens slowly after a substantial breach, and any further lapse takes the progress immediately back to zero – or maybe below.

On most nights Susan went to bed in the master bedroom alone before Mark retired to the guest room. Mark often stayed up on the computer well past midnight. One morning after Mark had left for work, Susan logged on to the computer to discover Mark's failure to cancel out of the internet porn site he had been viewing the night before. She was crushed.

On one end of the continuum, you have the lapses that arise from neglect. In these situations, your partner's needs haven't risen to a level of importance to be greater than your own. It's a form of selfishness. On the other end of the continuum, lack of accountability plays out in the form of lying, deception, secretiveness, or infidelity. These breaches do lasting damage.

> *Without knowing any of the details of Mark's interest and activity with pornography, she felt like her husband was cheating on her. His lack of interest in the bedroom now had context. With her best effort to remain open minded, Susan braced herself for a confrontation.*

In an effective connection, partners consistently follow through with commitments. When people struggle with accountability, they are communicating a lack of interest and value in the other person.

Most of us have some tolerance for an occasional lapse. We all drop the ball every once in a while. Things happen and priorities shift. We get busy and our responsibilities are spread thin. Forgetting to take care of a detail or missing a deadline can happen when we are overwhelmed, and some things can slip through the cracks.

Relationship accountability, however, involves a deep commitment to another person. This is a measure of your integrity. When you make a commitment in the context of a relationship, you are giving your word – an extension of yourself. Accountability breaches in relationships can weaken the fabric of a connection. A broken promise is like telling someone you don't care enough about them to make them a priority in your life.

Big or small, we all make mistakes. Take ownership of your action or omission and work with your partner to decide how best to move forward. What you do next defines intent. Conversations that support accountability in a relationship start with key questions:

- What is the best way for us to ensure reliability, dependability, and follow-through?
- How can I own responsibility when I have let someone down?

Susan and Mark had a great deal to fix after the trust had been broken in their relationship. The starting point was Mark's willingness to own accountability for his actions. If he was able to own up to his choices, Susan was prepared to find a way to understand his decisions and seek whatever resources were needed to move their relationship to a better place.

In a successful Intimacy stage, couples allow their connection to grow by practicing respect and holding themselves and each other accountable for the consequences of their choice to risk the vulnerability of closeness.

Challenges of the Adventure Stage

Challenge #7: Risk

Seth was single when he began his quest to become a professional musician. For the first decade or so, he worked long hours and made very little money. He was following his dream, but the late nights and artist lifestyle were taking their toll. Cara met Seth at a library while they were both searching the music racks for jazz CDs. Her nine-to-five lifestyle created challenges when she tried to last through Seth's third set and help him break down his equipment following a show.

In time, they found a rhythm that eventually led to a decision to commit to a long-term relationship. As a young couple, life was exciting, and they were making enough money between them to pay their bills and finance Cara's evening graduate school classes.

After they married and welcomed their first child, Seth's hours and lifestyle began to create an imbalance in their relationship. Most of the childcare and domestic responsibilities were being assumed by Cara, because Seth was either practicing or performing during the majority of his waking hours. He had a dream to make it big in the music industry. While Cara supported that dream, the business of running a family and navigating her own career was difficult.

Partnerships that evolve find comfort when moving into new areas and experimenting with new ideas. When people struggle with risk, they are often either reacting to past events or are anticipating the most negative consequences of the chance they are about to take.

Worry and anxiety are the body's way of telling us there might be danger ahead. Often, we are worrying about something that has not happened and probably never will. Regardless, it is normal to experience caution whenever you stretch your limits or try something new. The healthy apprehension that reminds you of the consequences usually gets mixed with the fun and excitement of anticipation.

When two people embark on a risk together, decisions are driven by either the most fearless or most fearful member of the relationship. Fearless partners push their apprehensive counterparts forward. Fearful partners pull their more confident partners back. This dynamic push and pull generates creative tension in the relationship that forces either growth or stagnation. Ideally, the tension creates a system of checks and balances allowing the couple to move forward at just the right speed. Sometime all we need to do is recognize the tension so we can approach the process with awareness of the consequences and sensitivity to our partner's experience.

The symptoms most likely to appear when risk is being negotiated represent both the eagerness for and the resistance to the consequences of the change. If the more fearful partner is pulling, the couple will be affected by issues like resistance to change, fear of failure, or a simple lack of resources. If the more fearless partner is pushing, the couple will be influenced by feeling over-extended, daring, or "out on a limb." Of course, both fearlessness and fearfulness have value, depending on what's at stake.

> One night, Cara and Seth sat down and weighed their options. Two things were clear. First, if Seth were to continue to pursue his dream, the wellness of their relationship and the health of their family were likely to suffer. Second, if they were to redefine their goals to support the health and wellness of the family, Seth's career path would have to change.
>
> For hours, they compared and contrasted the pros and cons of each path. Eventually, they located a compromise that they could both accept. Seth's music career could potentially thrive in a different way if he took on more teaching and recording assignments in exchange for less late-night performing. While he was

less likely to "make it big," the trade-off of choosing a less risky lifestyle was worth it.

Taking smart risks brings excitement and adventure to the life of a relationship. Much like driving a car, you are less likely to take a risk if you have passengers on board than if you are traveling alone. In relationships, risk-taking must account for the consequences on all parties involved.

This balance creates one of the greatest challenges of the relationship, as partners blend their personalities to move forward as one while honoring the needs of each individual. Conversations that support smart risk-taking in relationships start with key questions:

- What is our appetite for adventure and change? What are we willing to risk? What are we not?
- Are we willing to endure and learn from the pain that typically accompanies growth?

Seth and Cara were willing to try something new to meet a set of challenges they hadn't anticipated. They accepted the discomfort that came with the commitment to change, even though the outcome wasn't guaranteed.

Challenge #8: Leveraging Difference

In the Miller family, you were valuable if you were an athlete. Both parents, Carmen and Stacy, were stellar athletes throughout high school and college. Their children seemed to have inherited the same gifts. Both Carmen and Stacy coached their three children's sports teams. In a community of less competitive parents, Miller-coached teams usually won games and league championships. Most of the other parent-coaches wanted Miller kids on their teams, but hated to face them when they populated the opponent's teams. The parents' competitive passion for athletics had become their strongest marital bond.

When the Miller's eldest son, Luke, reached high school, the level of conflict between him and his father grew more intense than experienced by a typical 14-year-old. From Carmen's perspective, Luke had stopped playing hard. On the ride home following a particularly bitter loss, Carmen barked for about 20 uninterrupted minutes on how Millers don't give up and how Millers never quit. He was ashamed of Luke. Needless to say, Luke had grown distant from his father. Conversations were all one-sided.

In the spring of his freshman year in high school, Luke decided not to try out for the baseball team. In an awkward dinner conversation, he announced he was going to audition for a part in the theatre department's upcoming musical performance. The table went silent. Carmen threw down his fork and abruptly left the table.

Thriving relationships value and encourage different perspectives to promote growth. When people struggle with differences, it is often an inability to consider an alternate perspective to their own. There is more than one right answer to most questions. Sociologists use the term "equifinality" to describe how many paths can lead to the same destination. Unfortunately, many relationships are ruled by an approach that gives power to one partner while removing it from the other.

The sad result of this power play is the relationship's ability to change becomes limited by having only one opinion. All other possibilities are disabled even if they might create more resources, less cost, greater learning, better efficiency, stronger growth, or simply increase the fun and excitement in the relationship. Differences, by their nature, increase the pool of options. They add more colors to the palette. They elevate more ideas for consideration.

Appreciating another perspective means understanding what would need to be true for the other person's view to make sense. Perhaps you would feel the same way if you were in similar circumstances. More importantly, valuing differences invites two brains, two perspectives, two histories, and two sources of creativity to every conversation.

By the end of the meal, only Stacy and her frightened son were left at the dinner table. Stacy breathed a deep sigh and then asked Luke to tell her more about the theatre audition. He looked up as though he was surprised she was taking an interest.

Slowly, Luke revealed that many of his friends had commented on how well he sang and had encouraged him to audition. He added that, ever since he was a little boy, he had wanted to play guitar like his Uncle Will (Stacy's brother). He said that music was the only thing that made him excited. He confessed he even thinks about music when he's playing sports. Smiling, Stacy assured him that he had her support and that, although it might take some time, his father would eventually come around.

Later that night, Stacy implored Carmen to have an open mind. She urged him to rethink his biases and stereotypes. She reminded him that her brother, Uncle Will, was one of Carmen's best friends, despite being kind of "artsy." She asked him to imagine what it would have been like had his parents failed to value his athletic gifts and instead forced him to prioritize his academics. She suggested that he put himself in Luke's shoes for a moment.

Leveraging difference is the ultimate show of respect toward a relationship partnership. Communicating appreciation for a perspective other than your own informs your partner that their thoughts, feelings, and ideas are important to you.

When you deliver this message, a similar level of respect is usually returned. The goal is not to persuade the other to your viewpoint. The goal is for both partners to understand each other's perspective and then leverage that understanding to decide how best to move forward.

When partners behave as though their perspective is the only way to view events, they lose the advantage of partnering. Conversations that leverage differences in relationships start with key questions:

- What are the aspects of my partner's strengths and abilities that best balance mine?
- How can we, as partners, best capitalize on our differences?

The Miller family marriage had been weakened by a single-minded focus on sports. It could be enriched by the discovery that artistic and athletic talents can co-exist. The lesson of their oldest son's bravery might lead them to better understand the uniqueness of each member of the family.

In a successful Adventure stage, couples stretch themselves to explore new territory and embrace the feeling of risk that comes from capitalizing on their differences.

CHALLENGES OF THE SPACE STAGE

Challenge #9: Mourning

Theresa and Vic had only dated for a few months when he was deployed to Afghanistan. During the height of the war, their exchanges were infrequent, yet the long-distance conversations somehow drew them closer together. After two years of phone calls and emails, they shared a bond that had survived both time and distance. Marriage was now a topic of most conversations. However, the prolonged absence of seeing each other was weighing on them.

Losses take many forms. In a healthy connection, partners are able to acknowledge change that has taken place and can cope with their feelings related to the change. When people struggle with loss, they may be sad and overwhelmed. It is difficult to attend to the needs of others when depleted from sadness. Lovers can have trouble with intimacy because it's natural to become internally focused when feeling hurt.

The news that Vic would be returning for a second tour of duty made the trip home all too brief. Theresa anticipated his arrival with urgency as she wondered how they would keep the momentum of their connection moving forward. She wanted to be married to Vic but struggled to imagine another two years of not seeing each other, unreliable phone reception, delayed email replies, and deep loneliness.

Any relationship moves quickly to a defensive position when partners anticipate rejection or abandonment. Self-protection becomes a high priority. Because of the level of depletion, relationships are vulnerable to breaking down during these periods of transition. Quitting something can look like an easy and effective solution when compared to the labor of tolerating struggle. It's difficult to see the benefit of hanging in there when there's no energy to support that decision.

In his own way, Vic was unable to imagine the next two years either. Unbeknownst to Theresa, he had decided it was best to end the relationship. When Vic arrived at the airport to her embrace, Theresa could feel the distance in his hug. Something was wrong. The conversation was brief. Vic told Theresa that it was in both of their best interests to separate. He explained that he would be focused on daily survival and was unable to commit to the emotional requirements of a long-term relationship. Theresa made a meager attempt to get Vic to change his mind, but she could feel the certainty in his decision. They exchanged a tentative hug, endured a silent ride home from the airport, and went separate ways.

The initial reaction to a sudden disappointment is often exaggerated. It's a shock to the system. Current losses have a way of triggering the feelings from past losses. It is not uncommon for old, unresolved memories to get stirred up when we experience a loss, failure, or disappointment. For that reason, our reactions to loss are often larger than the events that trigger them. Therefore, it is important to acknowledge specifically what has changed and what is different. This helps to separate current challenges from past pressures that may still have a lingering effect.

Theresa spent the next three days in bed with the lights off and the curtains pulled shut. She called in sick to work and didn't answer emails, text messages, or phone calls. She cursed herself for falling so deeply in love with Vic and for allowing herself to be lulled into a sense of security about their future together. Theresa had never experienced a loss of this magnitude.

Eventually, Theresa answered the calls of her most

persistent and caring friends and family. She was soon surrounded by a circle of support as she endeavored to reestablish some normal rhythm in her life. Deep inside, she hoped the relationship with Vic wasn't really over. Perhaps his abrupt change was some sort of reaction to experiencing the trauma of war. Maybe he would call with a change of heart. Every time she allowed herself to imagine a reunion, the stark reality of her new circumstances set in. She had to find a way to move on with her life.

In time, energy returns to tackle the challenges of our new circumstances. Accepting the feelings of loss is the first step. Clarity follows in its own time. The exhaustion has purpose. It's designed to help you regroup so you can face the challenges of the new conditions ahead. Healthy relationships find a way to respect this process.

Mourning is the psyche's way of healing following an emotional injury. Partners can assist each other by appreciating how personal a loss may be and by allowing the person experiencing the loss to move at his or her own pace.

Conversations that help to support the need to mourn in relationships start with key questions:

- What is the historical context of the change? Have I lost a person, a thing, or my status?
- In what ways can I distance from the pain

temporarily to take care of life's responsibilities while I heal?

A near-loss has a way of teaching couples how to manage the sadness that fills each day. Vic and Theresa's lives went on. Whether the future would reunite them or keep them apart, each of them would now have to refocus their energy on the new circumstances their choices had created.

Challenge #10: Refocusing

Learning to walk all over again was not something Kim planned before entering her senior year of college. When her boyfriend, Chris, invited her on a trip to the lake for a summer afternoon of tubing and water skiing, neither of them foresaw the boating accident. When the flight-for-life helicopter transported her to the nearest medical trauma center, neither Kim nor Chris could have predicted the months of surgeries and years of rehab that were to come. Prior to the accident, the future seemed simple: date through college, graduate and get jobs, marry, and start a family. In one traumatic moment, everything changed.

Chris blamed himself for the accident. He didn't know how to make the situation better. Kim had moved beyond assigning blame for the accident. She was focused on reestablishing a life that didn't include her passions - running and mountain climbing. Although she had recovered beyond all of her doctors' expectations, there were certain things that would never again be possible as a result of the extent of her injuries. She was going to have to rethink her life plan.

Having acknowledged the loss, partners in strong relationships reset goals and work toward new challenges. When relationships struggle, new circumstances that have survived change may not always be accepted or understood. Many of the ground rules that governed the relationship in the past no longer apply. Each partner may have a different readiness to move forward. One partner may be slower to heal emotionally. In some cases, the new situation has produced very different visions for the future. Until there is a mutual readiness to turn the corner, the relationship will feel stuck. Partners move forward either apart or together.

Refocusing is a way of starting over. It removes the "what-ifs." Even if the eventual resolution is to dismantle the relationship, important decisions are best made after every reasonable effort has been made to address the challenges. If, in fact, the relationship moves forward, it inherits all the benefits of this work.

It's not necessary to wipe the slate completely clean. There are always important anchors that provide a place to begin. Learning how to move forward together following a significant loss requires a new phase of discovery. Different goals will strengthen the foundation. New conflicts will define day-to-day interactions. A greater level of intimacy will become possible.

> *For a long time, their relationship suffered from the aftermath of the injury. Communication was forced. The oppressiveness of the trauma made it hard to be lighthearted about anything. Neither Kim nor Chris had ever before managed such adverse circumstances. They considered separating as a way of achieving distance and perspective. They needed relief from the weight of what had happened to them. The emotions and realities that now occupied their thoughts were new and untested. It was like starting over.*

The choice to refocus sets the relationship's evolution in motion. It's like a new lease on life. The relationship has been gifted with an opportunity to redefine its direction. Any past struggles that were unresolved now have a chance to be addressed. This time, however, the partners bring the learning, tools, and resources that were acquired from their efforts to manage the most recent challenge. This, in turn, begins the next cycle of evolution in the relationship.

When relationships experience significant change, partners need to reassess their situation and reconsider their commitment to the future. If the relationship is going to move forward and thrive, a renewed energy will be required to rebuild the foundation. Conversations that help relationships refocus on moving forward start with key questions:

- What is the nature of our new circumstances (e.g. addition/subtraction from the family, job change, health issues, stress/trauma)?
- How do we most productively direct our energy toward the new situation?

Adversity sometimes creates opportunities that would otherwise have not existed. Kim and Chris would need to forge new aspirations for their relationship because career and family goals will now be shaped by the outcome of Kim's medical recovery. The relationship will now need to operate with new rules, roles, boundaries, and goals.

In a successful Space stage, couples distance from each other, physically or emotionally, to gain objectivity and perspective so they can take advantage of what has changed in order to move forward.

Summary

Norms, alignment, conflict, personal connection, respect, accountability, risk, leveraging difference, mourning, and refocusing. These are the ten vital anchors of strong relationships. Beginning in the Discovery phase, partners set their rules of engagement, find common direction, and learn how to disagree. As the Intimacy phase unfolds, partners practice considerate exchange as their closeness grows more warm and familiar. During the Adventure phase, the strength of this attachment allows the relationship to try new challenges and take advantage of the uniqueness of each partner. Finally, the Space phase allows partners to let go of what's changed and greet the new possibilities with fresh energy.

Of course, life rarely unfolds in a neat, clean sequence. Couples race through some stages and skip others. Sometime we progress and sometimes we regress. We take three steps forward and two steps back - or maybe two forward and three back. Occasionally things happen out of order. Our connections cycle through opportunity after opportunity to revisit vulnerabilities and convert them to strengths. We are frequently given new chances to give our connections a fresh look.

With each cycle, the connection can deepen. The lessons of growth enable more exciting discoveries. The bonds of togetherness explode with pleasure. The burst of intimacy energy dares exploration into new territories. Learning results and the cycle begins anew.

Afterward

Now What?

"How are we doing?"
"Fine, why do you ask?

"How are we doing?"
"Well…since you asked…"

What if everyone was accountable for their contribution to the health and wellness of every relationship they joined? Consider the consequence of more lasting friendships, more loving marriages, more satisfying affection, more productive problem solving, and more resilient adaptation to change.

Discovery, Intimacy, Adventure, and *Space*: these are the stages that foster healthy romantic relationships and keep them moving forward. At any moment, you can look at any relationship and ask where you are, why you are there, and what you should do to move in a positive direction. With every interaction, you can measure whether you've strengthened or weakened your connection. The opportunities are always there to guide your decisions.

Perhaps more than any other ability, the power to navigate interpersonal relationships with agility influences our quality of life. This is where we suffer our greatest pains and where we celebrate our most wondrous pleasures. There are no days off.

Every single interaction generates a negative or positive charge to the connection. For most of us, countless exchanges of relationship energy are transacted without thought or intention. For some of us, each altercation is a chance to strengthen a connection. Whether by overcoming an obstacle or taking action on a discovery, each day is full of opportunity.

Sustained relationships require sustained attention. In romance, it is always smart to ask, "So, how are we doing?" even when the answer is, "Fine, why do you ask?" Because eventually, the answer to the question will be, "Well...since you asked, I've been meaning to bring this up..." The more proactively you can detect and problem-solve the symptoms in a relationship, the less chance those symptoms will have to take root. Catch it early when the task is still manageable.

Embrace the struggles that accompany your connections. They have purpose. By owning your problems, you are able to engage with others in transformation and resolution. You just have to be willing to see that your struggles have a function. The purpose is growth. Cycle after cycle, we are invited to take our relationships to the next level.

Pain becomes useful and challenge becomes opportunity. The pain of misalignment dares you to compare values and goals. The pain of disagreement invites negotiation. The pain of accountability pushes maturity. The pain of risk ignites growth. The pain of loss enables renewal.

After reading this book, the next step is to engage in a self-assessment and discover the areas of your connections that need attention. A simple *card sort* exercise will unveil the relationship domains that have the greatest opportunities for change. When completed with your partner, conversations are ignited that demand attention. The Team Clock Interpersonal Assessment card sort can be found at **www.teamclock.com**.

You'll then need to make the time to have these conversations. Many couples don't see working on their relationship as a desirable way to spend their free time. But like any endeavor that requires nurturance and stewardship, the job is easier when approached proactively. An *action workbook* is also available as a guide for the work that lies ahead. The workbook poses the questions that are most likely to ignite healthy exchange between partners and provides a place to draft and document your action plan.

By collaborating in these discussions and capturing them in writing, you memorialize your commitment to the relationship and set milestones and timelines for the changes you wish to accomplish. Consequently, you move the relationship beyond the exercise of assessment and invigorate the decision to make measurable changes in the structure and dynamics of your day-to-day interactions.

This is not therapy. By choosing to look at the strengths and vulnerabilities of your relationship, you have not entered into professional counseling. You have merely chosen to invest more deeply in your relationships. If you need help beyond your own resources, find a qualified therapist. Some professional help can empower a couple with insights, tools, and resources needed to take ownership of their future. Check in on the **www.teamclock.com** website periodically to learn about upcoming Relationship Seminars and events you can attend with your loved one.

But there's plenty you can do on your own. Understand your history. Look for the themes and patterns that mark your most important relationships. Find the reason these themes exist. What purpose do they serve? What should you do next? What are you willing to change? This is the essence of self-help.

Relationships are complex, yet their cycles are simple and predictable. It takes a lot of strength to improve a relationship. Sadly, neglect is easier. Days pass and partners become comfortable with whatever level of connection has become normal. If you choose not to change, you sanction the decision to stall growth or remain stuck. Moving forward is often scary because it's unknown territory.

Now what? Perhaps you're in the midst of the wonder

that surrounds the amazing discovery of a new connection. Maybe you are dancing with the fire of intimacy. Perhaps you are gambling with adventure. Maybe your decision to create some space in the relationship has blossomed into clarity. Relationship challenges are as varied as the humans who create them.

Put your pain to use. Grasp each moment of each day with vigor. Savor each interaction in each relationship with novelty. Break through. Dare to be courageous. Taste discovery. Allow intimacy to work its magic. Taunt complacency. Appreciate adventure. Seize opportunities. Take smart risks. Learn from mistakes. Provoke change. Navigate space. Cherish loss. Heal with focus. Regroup. Advance with bravery. Evolve.

Acknowledgements

I am fortunate to be surrounded by family, friends, professional colleagues, and clients who teach me about the rich beauty of relationships every day. I am also lucky to live in a network of talented teammates who are completely comfortable in providing honest critique. This project has a significant piece of the following artists woven subtly into each paragraph.

Mawi Asgedom, A.P. Bartels, Ginger Barthel, Rachel Shaw Callahan, Jan Clavey, Amy Consolazio, Lu Dayment, Rich Dayment, Nikki Voda Donahue, Liz Driscoll, Michelle Mishler Frank, Jacki Fitzgerald Frederking, Kerry Galarza, Katy Gaughan, Aleksandra Gavrilovic, Alan Graham, Ph. D., Rev. Jeanne Hanson, Tina Haubert, Priscilla Herbison, Courtney Hunt, Ph. D., Eileen Joyce, Fr. Francis Kabiru, Nadine Kelly, M.D., Weykyoi Victor Kore, Erika Lindstrom, Randolph Lucente, Ph. D., Gail Meneley, Cara Milianti, Sarah Nun Moeri, Adam Nun, Patty Nun, Elvisa Pandzic, Pam Ohm-Pitock, Julianne Pedi, Carrie Peoples,

Caitlin Plank, Frank Portolese, Katie McDougall Powers, Mike Quinn, Meghan Ritter, Nancy Alexander Ritter, Ann Schreiner, Marie-Josée Shaar, Lisa Santucci Schvach, Valerie Scislowicz, David Taussig, Michael Wagner, M.D., Ragan Wilson, Tara Witt, and Joseph Zander, Ph. D..

Appendix

The Team Clock® Interpersonal Assessment Card Sort and Action Workbook are available at:
www.teamclock.com/interpersonalassessment

Inquiries about the Team Clock® Interpersonal Assessment or other Team Clock Institute products and services should be sent to:
info@teamclock.com

General information about the Team Clock Institute is available at:
www.teamclock.com

The Team Clock Institute offers an online assessment tool for teams in business, sports, education, and community settings at:
www.teamclockassessment.com

Clinical tools and resources for couples seeking professional counseling are available at:
www.centerforworkplaceinnovation.com

Made in the USA
Monee, IL
29 March 2023